The literary genetics of Shaw's most famous play are here examined for the first time. The sources of *Saint Joan* are closely compared with the original shorthand manuscript and that is compared with its subsequent revisions. This evidence is supplemented by facts drawn from Shaw's correspondence in print, in the British Library, and in private collections, and by accounts both in print and in the correspondence of people who knew Shaw at the time of his writing *Saint Joan*. The manuscript and its revisions are examined in the light of all that has been written about the play since it first appeared in 1923.

Tyson examines the events that led Shaw to write *Saint Joan*, establishes the times and places of its composition, and speculates on the "models" upon which Shaw may have based his heroine. The scene-by-scene investigation of the original manuscript accounts as far as possible for later alterations and revisions and discusses passages of critical or historical interest. The concluding chapters survey the circumstances surrounding the first production of the play in the United States, Great Britain, France, and Germany and reflect on the impact that *Saint Joan* has had on drama for more than half a century.

BRIAN TYSON teaches English at the University of Lethbridge. His numerous articles have appeared in such journals as *Modern Drama*, *The Shaw Review*, *Theatre Notebook*, *Shakespeare Quarterly*, and *Canadian Drama*.

The Story of Shaw's *Saint Joan*

Brian Tyson

McGill-Queen's University Press
Kingston and Montreal

© McGill-Queen's University Press 1982
ISBN 0-7735-0378-1
Legal deposit 2nd quarter 1982
Bibliothèque nationale du Québec

The author and publisher wish to thank the Society of Authors on behalf of the Bernard Shaw Estate for kind permission to quote previously published and unpublished extracts from *Saint Joan* by Bernard Shaw © 1982 The Trustees of The British Museum, The Governors and Guardians of The National Gallery of Ireland and Royal Academy of Dramatic Art.

This book has been published with the help of a grant from the Canadian Federation for the Humanities using funds provided by the Social Sciences and Humanities Research Council of Canada.

Printed in Canada

CANADIAN CATALOGUING IN PUBLICATION DATA

Tyson, Brian, 1933–
    The story of Shaw's Saint Joan
    Includes index.
    ISBN 0-7735-0378-1
    1. Shaw, George Bernard, 1856–1950. Saint Joan.
    2. Joan, of Arc, Saint, 1412–1431, in fiction,
    drama, poetry, etc. I. Title.
    PR5363.S33T97   822'.912   C81-095093-6

Cover illustration The sculpted head of St. Maurice, formerly in the Church of St. Maurice in Orleans, was traditionally supposed to have been modelled from Joan of Arc when she relieved the town. Shaw based the physical appearance of his heroine on the features of this sculpture. Reproduced by courtesy of the Musée Historique, Orleans.

Contents

Illustrations

Preface

Joan of Arc's dramatic pilgrimage began four hundred years ago with Shakespeare's unflattering portrait of her in *Henry VI*. Thereafter, for two hundred and fifty years, she was the romantic heroine of numerous plays, mostly jingoistic and melodramatic, even when leavened by the facts about her trial and rehabilitation made available by Quicherat in 1841. From this romanticism Bernard Shaw, with characteristic gallantry, rescued her in 1923, and set her on her feet again.

His achievement has, of course, been well recognized; and perhaps an apology is in order for presuming to add another book to the library of critical material already written about *Saint Joan*. It inspired two full-length books within a year of its first production, and since then has been the cause of literally hundreds of articles by distinguished scholars, among whom I cannot forbear mentioning Stanley Weintraub, whose introduction to his own edition of the play is but one of many fine pieces of work on *Saint Joan* by this scholar. My book, however, does not simply duplicate the work of others, though I hope I have assimilated all that these critics have had to tell me. Instead it seeks to do what has not been done before: to trace the development in Shaw's mind of his play about Joan of Arc; to follow his hand over the shorthand notebook in which he penned his first draft; to account for significant revisions to that script; to recapture the impact of the play's first appearance on the stages of the world; and briefly to estimate its continuing influence upon twentieth-century drama.

My point of departure was the original shorthand manuscript, British Library Add. MSS. 45923 (unless otherwise noted, parenthetical folio numbers refer to this manuscript). It was written in Pitman shorthand, and thus had to be transcribed; but the shorthand is remarkably clear (it is possible in places to decipher even heavily deleted passages), without contractions, and with only occasional errors. Shaw made a stroke for every consonant sound, and rarely used short forms. Proper nouns and "difficult" words (Champagne, for example) are written in longhand, but the characters' names are not capitalized as was his printed practice. Sometimes, it is difficult to distinguish between — (come) and — (go), and between · (a) and . (the), but the sense of the sentence is usually a determi-

nant. Between speakers Shaw inserts a paragraph sign, thus: ⌷ . This enables him
to continue interchange of dialogue along a single line instead of paragraphing
each speaker. For ease of reading I have set out the speakers as in a drama. Stage
directions he puts between square brackets, but not always in italics. He usually
underlines longer stage directions. To indicate a character speaking, Shaw uses =,
and I render it in the same way to distinguish it from the colon, for which he uses
the shorthand $\overset{x}{x}$. When, however, stage directions intervene, Shaw gives no sign
between the speaker and the dialogue:

> D'Estivet [throwing down his brief] My lord: do you need anything more than
> this?

To supplement the original shorthand there are a few sheets of corrected typescript (British Library Add. MSS. 50633, vol. 126 Saint Joan, 1923, Fragment,
autograph *longhand* and *typescript* with *autograph* corrections), Shaw claiming
to have destroyed the rest. From the full typescript was presumably printed the
so-called rough proof—unpublished, which is also in the British Library, with
interleaved corrections. Finally, there are the rehearsal copy in the Humanities
Research Center at the University of Texas and Shaw's Rehearsal Notes (British
Library Add. MSS. 50644, vol. 137) in the British Library.

Unless otherwise stated, the printed text of Shaw's play used is the first edition
published by Constable and Company, London, 1924. There are only one or two
minor revisions in the standard edition text of 1932.

In addition to Shaw's text I studied the unpublished correspondence of Shaw,
also in the British Library, and many other letters and postcards both by and to
him, which are in the possession of private owners, to obtain a picture of the way
he went to work; and, of course, I consulted every printed reference to Shaw's
play that I could find, including the newspaper accounts of early performances on
both sides of the Atlantic.

Acknowledgements

I have received a great deal of help in the preparation of my manuscript. In particular my thanks are due to the Canada Council, whose travel grant started me on my way and to Marilyn Gibboney, whose patient and skilful transcription of Shaw's shorthand provided much excitement in the early days. I am also grateful to the Society of Authors for permission to quote from the original manuscript, from Shaw's unpublished correspondence, and from the correspondence of Laurence Binyon and St. John Ervine; to Wilfred Blunt for permission to quote from Sir Sydney Cockerell's unpublished letter to Shaw, and to Edward Coleman for similar permission regarding a letter from Alfred Lord Douglas.

For the historical aspects of the study I am indebted to a number of distinguished and helpful correspondents, including Dr. Raymond Massey and Dr. Eva Le Gallienne, the Reverend James Murphy, C.M., of the Vincentian Community, and Father Kevin Condon, C.M., of All Hallows College, Dublin. Dame Margaret Cole, Dr. Philip Briggs, Philip Goode, and Eric Hankinson also provided much appreciated information.

1

From the Beginning

Underlying many of the guesses, when *Saint Joan* was first produced, as to why Shaw had written such a play, was a belief best summed up by the reviewer in the *Theatre Magazine* for March 1924, who spoke of "the remarkable change that has come over Mr. Bernard Shaw himself." According to this reviewer, in *Saint Joan* we are witnessing a "more kindly, humane Shaw." Saint Joan, concludes this critic, has wrought another miracle.

The nature of this "miracle" was succinctly stated by T. Michael Pope in the *Outlook* the following month: "Hitherto...each of Mr. Shaw's plays has been a challenge. *Saint Joan* is an acceptance."[1] But an acceptance of what? Pirandello, also in the first-night audience, had this to say in the *New York Times*: "From the epilogue of this drama on Joan of Arc we may gather almost explicitly the reason for which Mr. Shaw wrote it. This world, he seems to say, is not made for saints to live in. We must take the people in it for what they are, since it is not vouchsafed them to be anything else."[2] But it was G. K. Chesterton, three years later, who gave perspective to the "change" in Shaw, though, characteristically, he expressed it as a paradox:

> It is not a question of having reached a new stage, but of having found a new direction. He was born in the nineteenth century, impatient to plunge into the twentieth; perhaps thinking (like his own Mrs. Clandon) that he knew all about the twentieth. But by a resolute and real progress he has now advanced as far as the fifteenth....It would be an ungracious way of putting it to say that he has spent the first half of his life in running away from a religion and the second half in running after one. It would be much truer to say that he has spent the first half in unwinding a rope of convention or tradition and getting free from it; and the second half in looking for a rope (not necessarily the same rope) which should be strong enough to bind together again the bundle of life. In that sense he has done first one thing, and then the opposite; and has been undoing what he had done. But he was not necessarily wrong in this, or even inconsistent. It depends on knowing the ropes—or the religions.[3]

What did happen to start Shaw writing *Saint Joan* in 1923? Of course, as has been widely pointed out, his religious development had been continuous,[4] the atheism of the Irish immigrant slowly giving way to the mature dramatist's approval and espousal of a "mystic vitalism," which borrowed freely from the thinking of Carlyle, Shelley, Marx, Butler, Bergson, and Lamarck. And his plays reflect this development, just as they reveal his developing dramaturgy. Critics have seen structural foreshadowing of *Saint Joan*, for example, in other history plays such as *Caesar and Cleopatra* (1898) and *Annajanska: The Bolshevik Empress* (1917);[5] thematically, fore-echoes of the life of the saint appear in *Major Barbara* (1905),[6] *The Shewing up of Blanco Posnet* (1909),[7] and *Androcles and the Lion* (1911–12),[8] and more direct expressions of his Life Force theories take the stage, both forcibly discussed in *Man and Superman* (1901–3) and dramatically demonstrated in *Back to Methuselah* (1918–21). This last, a massive pentateuch, was Shaw's final attempt to state fully and urgently the religious needs of man as he saw them. Part myth, part science fiction, and part wish-fulfilment — not to say wishful thinking — it traces the evolution of man from the Garden of Eden, through this stormy century, and out as far as thought can reach. It may, indeed, have been further than most thought could reach in 1921. World War I had lowered the mental level of the age, and must have been a body blow to Shaw's evolutionary hopes, insofar as they depended upon man's perfectibility from within.

Perhaps a growing awareness of the deterioration of human society, from which the evolutionary process would have to operate, helped to turn Shaw's thinking outwards towards the possible intervention of God. For, like William James, with whose work he seems to have been familiar, Shaw believed not only in the "higher part" of a human being but in "the MORE of the same quality, which is operative in the universe outside of him,"[9] which Shaw called "Providence."[10] People of Joan's genius could make contact with the Life Force for the sake of others: it was necessary for society to be renewed, even if the saint had to be sacrificed. Joan's canonization, on 16 May 1920, threw her into public prominence and may well have caught Shaw's notice. Not only was she the kind of genius whom he had been representing dramatically for years, whose life was a drama ready-made; but the recognition of that genius five hundred years too late by the representatives of the very institution that had been instrumental in burning her presented an irresistible irony, and provided the opportunity of illustrating the fact that the forces to which Joan had been opposed were still very much alive in 1923.

In general terms one can agree with Susan Stone when she says, "In *Saint Joan* the focus of Shaw's attention is shifting from the heroic figure to the forces of humanity which constitute the hero's opposition."[11] And there is no doubt that the political manoeuvring immediately following the holocaust of World War I furnished Shaw with sufficient source material to fashion his antagonist. Indeed, Katherine Gatch is one critic who descried a motive for the writing of *Saint Joan* in Shaw's volume entitled *What I Really Wrote About the War* (1919),[12] particularly in the section "Peace Conference Hints" where Shaw warns of the "greed and rancor which abuse victory" and then states: "There is only one force that can beat both; and that force is the entirely mystic force of evolution applied through the sort of living engine we call the man of principle." When those words were written, the "man" in question was President Wilson; and Shaw goes on to warn that if he fails, Europe will inevitably find herself at war again; or, throwing democratic parliaments to the winds, try dictatorships, and even international chaos and anarchy in order that they may work out their natural remedy. As Gatch points out, by the time Shaw came to write *Saint Joan*, Wilson *had* failed — indeed was dead. Other critics, too, have seen the genesis of Shaw's drama in the play of power politics following World War I. Even some theatre critics who attended the play's opening night were sensitive to its echoes of contemporary politics. Jack Crawford, for example, makes an immediate and cynical connection between the thirteenth and the twentieth centuries:

> Now the world is conducted by organizations, governments, feudal systems, and what not, that are ill-prepared to face a test of merciless logic. Such organizations are vast and powerful machines whose motive power is self-interest, the leadership of the few at the expense of the many. Once permit the many to know the truth, and the illogical domination of the few would be in danger. So all organizations are a conservative force whose primary object is not truth but self-perpetuation.[13]

There seems little doubt that Shaw would have applauded that conclusion: in his unreleased statement to New York theatre audiences, written on 3 January 1924, Shaw mentions his interest in the people's want of any grasp of the political forces that move civilizations. Clearly, he does delight in probing the problems of government; and the political forces taking shape in Europe after World War I excited his concern, and made the persecution of the individual conscience most appropriate material for Shaw's pen.

In addition to Shaw's spiritual and political development, two other events in his personal life in the years immediately preceding the writing of *Saint Joan* might have triggered him into action. The first was a letter from his old friend and one-time collaborator, William Archer, in which he suggested that Shaw's influence was less than it had been twenty years before. The reason, according to Archer, was that "your public (small blame to them) declines to take you seriously." He exhorts him to "Let us for once, or twice, or thrice, have the gold without the slag; working it into whatever artistic form you please. Say, for instance, a great play, realistic or symbolic, that should go to every city in the world and shake the souls of people instead of their midriffs."[14] The second was his association with Father J. Leonard, C.M.[15]

This remarkable priest, who, in addition to Shaw, numbered among his friends such eminent men as G. K. Chesterton, Desmond MacCarthy, Abbot Butler, James A. Costello (Prime Minister of Ireland) and President John F. Kennedy,[16] received many friendly visits from the Shaws while he was living in Horace Walpole's old house at Strawberry Hill, Twickenham, during the twenties. When Shaw came to write *Saint Joan*, Father Leonard acted as "technical advisor," providing Shaw with facts, suggestions, and finally criticism. According to Denis Gwynn, they disagreed over Shaw's interpretation of the saint: "Shaw's thesis in his play Saint Joan was that she was a rebel against the Church's dictation, whereas Father Leonard tried to make him understand that time after time, she was appealing to Rome as the supreme authority against her local critics."[17] Elsewhere, Gwynn says that "there are letters surviving in which Shaw writes that if they continue their discussions it will end in Shaw being the defender of the Catholic Church with Fr. Leonard as the apologist for Protestantism."[18] Unfortunately, the letters in question were disposed of by Leonard to some of his friends before he died,[19] so it is impossible to reconstruct the overall discussion mentioned above; but Shaw evidently appreciated keenly the advice and argument he received, for he "presented Fr. Leonard with his own autographed proofs of the play."[20]

That Shaw had been considering the Catholic saint as a likely heroine for his next play (certainly by the late autumn of 1922) is attested by a letter to him from Father Leonard, from which it appears that Shaw had recently read with interest the life of Dominic Plater[21] at the behest of the Irish priest whose purpose, he declares, was to let Shaw see "that the Church is large enough to contain all sorts of queer fish."[22] The letter then goes on to give a detailed explanation, obviously in answer to Shaw's request, of the nature of the trial of Joan of Arc. Already a quarrel seems to be developing along the lines suggested by Denis Gwynn above:

> I would demur to your description—and in this I should expect to be supported by all instructed Catholics—of the trial being "merciful and fair under the circumstances." I would describe it as illegal and unjust. Cauchon was clearly out for her death. As an example take what he said after her retractation [sic], to the English "We shall get her yet."

Father Leonard concludes with the request that Shaw "control all my statements by reference to Quicherat.... You may possibly get it in the London Library. The Procès is translated, if not the whole, then a good part of it in a book called Jeanne d'Arc—the Story of her life by Murray."[23] According to Sir Sydney Cockerell, Shaw already had a copy of T. Douglas Murray's book:

I have always been under the impression that I was in a small way responsible for St. Joan by giving you or introducing you to Douglas Murray's book containing the full proceedings at her trial and rehabilitation and suggesting that you might do something with it—but perhaps I am mistaken. This book filled me with excitement when it appeared and I gave copies to each of my children, as well as to some of my friends.[24]

But perhaps it was Father Leonard who sent him back to it; or perhaps Archibald Henderson is correct when he states that Cockerell brought Shaw the copy of Murray early in 1923,[25] in which case it was either a most fortunate coincidence, or at Shaw's request, following Father Leonard's letter.

In the light of the above, the following statement by Norman Carrington, made in 1950, can be seen to be a misleading oversimplification: "The Play was obviously occasioned by Joan's canonization in 1920."[26] Yet the same statement was repeated by no less a critic than F. S. Boas the following year.[27] Another common oversimplification of the genesis of Saint Joan derived from Shaw himself, and his wife Charlotte, who, according to Hesketh Pearson in his 1942 biography, persuaded her husband to tackle the Saint Joan theme. The story is perhaps best told by John Mason Brown, who states:

> Yet apparently he resisted Joan as a theme and would have continued to do so had not Charlotte Shaw employed strategy to get her husband started on a play she wanted him to write. Being a good wife . . . she did not argue with Shaw or let him feel that she was influencing him. Instead she left books about the Maid and her trial around the house in places where he was certain to see them, pick them up and read them in his moments of idleness. He fell for the bait and, once having fallen, became absorbed in Joan.[28]

The same year Shaw's secretary, Blanche Patch, repeated the story;[29] and five years later it was elaborated upon by St. John Ervine, who dramatized it a little more, pointing up Charlotte's "strategy" and Shaw's ignorance of the way he was being manipulated.[30] In 1964 Saint Joan's first director, Lawrence Langner, told the story again, claiming he had it from Mrs. Shaw herself.[31] And in 1968 J. W. Miller varied it a little by having Cockerell make his gift of Quicherat's Procès to Charlotte Shaw, thus increasing her part in the fable, and diminishing her husband's.[32] She, according to Miller, "got Shaw to look at the book with noncommittal response." He then repeats the story of her leaving "many different books" about Joan of Arc lying about.

It is not for me to quarrel with the details of the above anecdote: no doubt Charlotte believed she was responsible for suggesting the play to Shaw's mind, and perhaps she was instrumental in getting him started on it; but the story of her coercion and his resistance obscures a more important truth: namely, Shaw's own vivid interest in linking past and present events, and the development of his religious beliefs; in short, his personal pilgrimage towards *Saint Joan*.

Once the decision had been taken and the research done some time in the late autumn of 1922, precisely when and where did Shaw write *Saint Joan*? Shaw himself, to settle a dispute which had arisen on Radio Eireann "Question Time" as to whether the play had been written at Glengariff or Parknasilla, wrote to the *Irish Independent* as follows:

> I wrote it in 1923. During that year I was at Glengariff from the 18th July to the 15th August, and at Parknasilla from the 15th August to the 18th September working at the play all the time. . . . But the play was neither begun nor finished in Eire. A good deal of it was written in rapidly moving trains between King's Cross and Hatfield on the London, Midland and Scottish Railway; and to locate this part of it is a problem in Cartesian geometry which I leave to Mr. de Valera, as he is an expert in mathematics and I a hopeless duffer.[33]

Shaw, however, has been known to be in error when dating his own work. He it was who perpetrated the curious error that he began his first play, *Widowers' Houses*, in 1885, instead of 1884. This carelessness, refutable by reference to Shaw's diary and the original manuscript, has been repeated by nearly all his critics and biographers, leading to the implication that when writing *Widowers' Houses*, Shaw dramatized the facts of the Royal Commission on the Housing of the Working Classes, the findings of which were not available to him until nine months after he had completed two acts of his play. That Shaw's letter, cited above, contains a statement in direct contradiction to another of his statements adds to one's caution; for the letter concludes with the following list of "birthplaces" of *Saint Joan*: "And I visited not only Glengariff and Parknasilla, but made some stay at Bournemouth, Minehead, Malvern, Stratford-upon-Avon, Birmingham and Oxford: ten birthplaces in all." Yet, in answer to an earlier questionnaire put to him by Leslie Rees, Shaw had emphatically denied that he wrote any of *Saint Joan* in Stratford, saying: "I did not write a line of it in Stratford. Most of it was written in County Kerry, in Ireland. You forget that Shakespeare is still held responsible for the first part of 'Henry VI,' with its infamous libel on Joan. She would have risen from the Seine and punched my head if I had penned her name in Stratford."[34] And Blanche Patch, Shaw's secretary for thirty years, and for whom *Saint Joan* was the first, and therefore the most important, play she transcribed for him, saw Ireland exclusively as the place of composition: "G.B.S. went off to County Kerry to write *Saint Joan*."[35] In spite of these conflicting accounts, the truth can be readily arrived at. Not only is the original shorthand manuscript extant, and the dates and places of composition of most of the scenes written thereon, but this information is amplified by Shaw himself in his accompanying letter to the director of the British Museum on 2 June 1944. Here he sets out a rough timetable of the writing of *Saint Joan*, which we can correct and complete from the original manuscript and a reading of his correspondence for the year 1923.

From this last we learn that on 28 March 1923 the Shaws left Ayot St. Lawrence for a circular tour through several counties. They planned to spend the first night at Oxford, and lunch the following day with Lillah McCarthy.[36] By 5 April they were at the Hotel Metropole, Minehead, Somerset, whence Shaw wrote to Molly Tompkins that they intended to stay for a week or two, "potter about in the old car until we go to Stratford on the 30th."[37] On 9 April, Shaw wrote to Lawrence Langner telling him that he had written an article on the need for a new theatre, and that he was "sending it to London today to be typed from my shorthand."[38] The article in question, though it remained unpublished until it appeared in *Theatre Magazine* in May 1925, is a further aid to the dating of *Saint Joan*, since it reveals that by the above-quoted date Shaw had in mind the shape his play was going to take, if not its final length:

> My next play will be a chronicle play which will be impracticable without a Shakespearean stage. I do not know whether it will be in fifty scenes or fifteen or five hundred; but in writing it I shall ignore the limitations of the XIX century stage as completely as Shakespear did. I shall have to depend on the Theatre Guild of America for a performance of it, just as I had to depend on it for a performance of Back to Methuselah.[39]

By 27 April the Shaws were at the Malvern Hotel, Great Malvern, and from here Shaw wrote again to Molly Tompkins: "I am beginning a new play after all— another historical one."[40] In the account that accompanied his original manuscript to the British Museum, Shaw twice stated that he began the play on 29 April at Great Malvern. Molly Tompkins claimed that it was at Stratford-on-Avon that Shaw first announced that he was going to write about Joan of Arc "to save her from Drinkwater!" And, according to the manuscript itself, he finished his first scene at Stratford-on-Avon, though the date given is "4 April 1923"! This should presumably be 4 May. The manuscript states that he began Scene II back at Ayot St. Lawrence on 9 May and finished it there on the twentieth. The Loire Scene (Scene III)[41] was finished at Ayot St. Lawrence three days later, and the Tent Scene (Scene IV)[42] was also finished at Ayot on 6 June. We have no information about the place and time of the beginning of Scene V,[43] but know that it was concluded at Ayot on the twenty-fourth of the same month. The Trial Scene (Scene VI)[44] again has no opening date, but its ending is clearly marked "Adelphi Terrace, 12/7/23." How much of the play had been put into typescript by his

new secretary, Miss Patch, before Shaw left for Ireland on 18 July, it is impossible
to tell; but that he took with him as much as had been transcribed, to correct it,
can be taken as a matter of course. At the beginning of the Epilogue (Scene VII),
in the original manuscript, occurs the date 6 August 1923; and Shaw, in his
accompanying note to the director of the British Museum, confirms that this part
of his play was begun at Glengariff, Co. Cork, on that date, when Shaw was
staying at the Eccles Hotel. By 17 August he was at the Great Southern Hotel,
Parknasilla-on-Sea, Co. Kerry, whence he wrote to Mary Hankinson[45] to explain
why he must miss the Fabian Summer School that year:

> I had arranged to leave my wife here and carry out an elaborate program at
> Hindhead, Birmingham (to rehearse Methuselah), Oxford (Heartbreak House)
> and Bath (to unveil a tablet to Sheridan). But with a dock strike on, plus an
> election, plus a threatened general strike, leaving one's wife is not so easy;
> not that the place is not perfectly quiet—one would suppose that a shot had
> never been fired or a house burnt—but because travellers have to carry their
> own luggage, and I do not quite see Charlotte boarding the steamer with a
> trunk on each shoulder, a hatbox on her head, a bursting holdall under each
> arm and a kitbag on her little finger.
>   Besides, I see that I must stay here until I finish my Joan of Arc play, and
> let everything else go smash, including Methuselah, which the Birmingham
> people must produce as best they can.[46]

A week later, on 24 August, following the words "The End" on the manuscript,
Shaw wrote the completion date and place, Parknasilla. And on 27 August he
wrote to Molly Tompkins, "Saint Joan is finished (except for the polishing): a mag-
nificent play; and I thought I should never write another after Methuselah!"[47]
    We are left with Blanche Patch's statement that "G.B.S. went off to County
Kerry to write Saint Joan"; and Shaw's own puzzling and twice-repeated assertion
in the notes accompanying his manuscript that the Trial Scene was written at
Parknasilla: "The Trial Scene must have been finished at Parknasilla, as I remember reading it there to Fathers Leonard and Sheehy."[48] The operative word in that
sentence is "finished": fortunately we have more corroborative evidence in the
eighteen pages of original corrected typescript that remain (the rest, according to
Shaw's accompanying note, were torn up at Ayot on 8 February 1926), which
complete the picture. Evidently, Shaw left England to complete the play in
County Kerry, taking with him Blanche Patch's typed transcript of the shorthand
he had already given her (and perhaps receiving more by post). He corrected the
transcript and returned it to her in London, at the same time as he was writing the
first draft of the Epilogue. On the first page of Act I in this typescript, duly
corrected, we have Shaw's longhand injunction: "Proofs to Bernard Shaw Park-

nasilla, Kenmore, Co. Kerry, Ireland if posted before the 12th September 1923. If later, to 10 Adelphi Terrace, London W.C.2." Shaw here was revising his work in Ireland for the printer. A time allowance for mail to cross the Irish Sea accounts for the date he mentions, which is six days before his projected return to England on 18 September. Another stray date on the typescript confirms that Shaw finished his revision of Scene II on 3 September, at Parknasilla. The last page of the Trial Scene in typescript proves that it was indeed originally finished in England (at Adelphi Terrace), while Shaw's autograph corrections, presumably made in Ireland, mean that the manuscript was finished there in another sense (which settles Blanche Patch's comment), and could well have been read at that time to the two priests, as Shaw himself remembered. On 12 September, writing from Parknasilla, Shaw reminded Molly Tompkins that next week he would be at the Malvern Hotel, Great Malvern, adding that "Saint Joan is finished, except for revision and arrangement of the stage business."[49] And apparently *Saint Joan* ended where it had begun, for the last words on the final typewritten sheet of the Epilogue are "Revision for press finished at Malvern, 28/9/23."

Sculpted head of St. Maurice, once
thought to be of Joan of Arc.

Mary Hankinson

T. E. Lawrence

Sybil Thorndike as "The Maid"

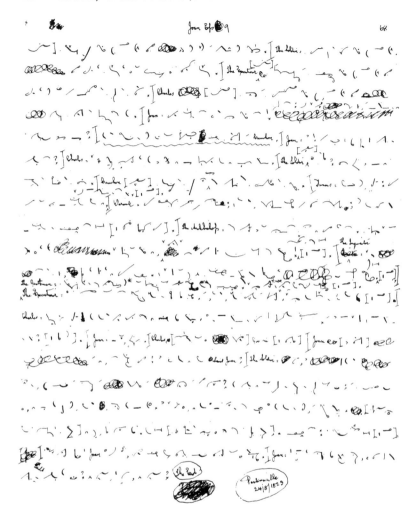

Saint Joan: the end of the Epilogue. British Library Add. MSS. 45923, *Saint Joan* shorthand, fol. 68

SAINT JOAN ~~STAGE~~

A C T I

7 ~~²~~   *3*

February 23rd, 1429 :

~~On a bright April day~~ a fine spring morning on the river Meuse, between Lorraine and Champagne.

Captain Robert de Baudricourt, a ~~military young~~ soldier and gentleman with more energy than he can work
off in the routine of his military command and house-
keeping *in the castle of* ~~the~~ Vaucouleurs, is expending its superfluity in
storming at his steward, a trodden worm, scanty of flesh,
scanty of hair, who might be any age from 18 to 55, being the sort of man *whom* ~~that~~ age cannot wither because he
has never bloomed.

The two are in a plain stone chamber *on the first floor* of the castle.
~~illuminated~~ At a *plain* strong oak table, seated in ~~an oaken~~
~~captain's~~ chair *to match,* the captain *presents his* left profile. ~~in view.~~ The
steward stands facing him at the other side of the table,
if *to* ~~his~~ depr*e*catory *stance,* ~~e~~ ~~a~~ *as his* can be called standing. The
unglazed thirteenth century window is behind him; and
near it in the corner is a turret with a narrow arched
doorway *leading to a winding stair which descends to the courtyard. There is a*
stout four-legged stool under the table.

ROBERT   No eggs! No eggs!! Thousand thunders, man, what
do you mean by no eggs?

STEWARD   Sir: it is not my fault. It is the act of God.

ROBERT   Blasphemy. You tell *me* that there are no eggs; and
you blame *your Maker* ~~God~~ for it.

STEWARD   Sir: what can I do? I cannot lay eggs.

ROBERT   (sarcastic) Ha! You jest about it.

Saint Joan: the opening of Scene I. British Library Add. MSS. 50633, vol. 126, Fragment
autograph *longhand* and *typescript*, fol. 3

26.   7

What is my business? Helping mother at home. What is thine? Petting lapdogs and sucking sugarsticks. I call that muck. I tell thee it is God's business we are here to do: not our own. I have a message to thee from God; and thou must listen to it, though thy heart break with the terror of it.

CHARLES   I don't want a message; but can you tell me any se-
crets? Can you do any cures? Can you turn lead into
gold, or anything of that sort?

JOAN   I ~~promise~~ can turn thee into a king, in Rheims cathedral ~~; and that is a miracle that will take some doing, it seems~~.

CHARLES   If we go to Rheims, and have a coronation, Anne will
want new dresses, which we can't afford. I am all
right as I am. *How are less than my father's poorest shepherd as you are.*
JOAN   You are not the lawful owner of your own land, *of thine* until
you are consecrated.

CHARLES   I shall not be the lawful owner of, *my own land* anyhow. Will
the consecration pay off my mortgages? I have pledged
my last acre to the Archbishop and the Constable. I
owe money even to Bluebeard. ~~~~

JOAN

Charlie: I come from the land, and have gotten my strength from working on the land; and I tell thee that the land is there to rule righteously and keep God's peace; and not to pledge at the pawnshop as a drunken woman pledges her children's clothes. And I come from God to tell thee to kneel in the

cathedral and solemnly give your kingdom to Him for ever
and ever, and become *the greatest king in the world* as his steward and trustee,
his soldier and his servant. It's very clay *will* ~~~~
become holy: *the soldiers will be the soldiers of God:* the rebel dukes ~~~~ rebels
against God; the English *will* ~~~~ fall on their *knees*
and beg you to let them return to their lawful homes in peace. Wilt thou be a poor little Judas and betray me and Him that sent me?

Saint Joan: from Scene II. British Library Add. MSS. 50633, vol. 126, Fragment autograph *longhand* and *typescript*, fol. 7

2

The Maid and Her Miracles

As a model for his saint, Shaw was allegedly impressed by at least three of his contemporaries when he wrote *Saint Joan*. The first and best known of these was Dame Sybil Thorndike, the actress, who had been his friend since 1908 when she had understudied for the part of Candida in a touring company. According to Shaw's wife Charlotte, it was after he saw Sybil Thorndike play Hecuba in *The Trojan Women* in 1919 that he announced, "I am going home to write *Saint Joan*."[1] In fact, however, he didn't: instead he went home and continued writing *Back to Methuselah*. Others maintain that it was her performance in another play that spurred Shaw into action. In 1922 Sybil Thorndike and her husband Lewis Casson were invited to associate themselves with Lady Wyndham and Bronson Albery in the management of the New Theatre; here they decided to present, among other plays, Shelley's tragedy *The Cenci*. Russell Thorndike, writing about his sister, says:

> I believe it is true that Shaw chose Sybil [for Joan] after he'd seen her in the trial scene of Beatrice Cenci—at least, I've read that in the newspapers, so it's probably so, and confirms what she and Lewis have always said, that when they do a show simply for love of it, and not bothering whether anyone likes it or not, something good always comes of it, and certainly this good did come to Sybil.[2]

Sybil Thorndike herself, recalling events for Hesketh Pearson in 1942, claimed: "It was after the trial scene, I think, that Mr. Shaw said he had found the actress for Joan."[3] And Dame Sybil's obituary in *The Times* of London (10 June 1976) repeats this information. The first performance of *The Cenci* was on 13 November 1922.

A hint that his decision may have been taken earlier than the run of *The Cenci* is also to be found in Russell Thorndike's book:

Now some months before, news had come that Bernard Shaw was writing a play on Joan of Arc, and Sybil was in a fever lest she should not be allowed to play it.

I believe another writer was already at work on a Joan play for her, but of course Shaw was beyond her wildest dreams. She wrote, or probably it was Lewis who wrote, as Sybil has some absurd plan she works on of never interfering with Fate; anyway, one of them wrote—they can't remember which—and asked Shaw outright who was going to play it, and he wrote back saying that of course Sybil was going to play it, and that if anyone else happened to be writing the play for her, she could give it to another actress to do, for she had got to play his Saint Joan.[4]

Unfortunately, since neither Shaw's letter nor the one from Sybil Thorndike (or her husband) has survived, the "some months before" must remain just that; but the other author who was writing a "Joan" play for Sybil Thorndike was Laurence Binyon, who had been commissioned by the Cassons to write it. According to Sheridan Morley, when Binyon heard about Shaw's play he "gracefully withdrew from the conflict."[5] Shaw was not interested in attributes of youth: Sybil Thorndike was forty in 1922; but he had no doubt watched her mature from playing in light farce, through mature comedy to tragedy; and her performance as Beatrice Cenci must have confirmed for Shaw the rightness of his decision. *The Times* review of her performance in Shelley's play makes this clear:

> Miss Thorndike's acting, which falters while terror possesses Beatrice, attains a strength and beauty which we have not before seen in it when the fatal decision is once taken. It thus happens that, in those later passages when Beatrice's hardness in face of her deed is most likely to estrange her from the audience, Miss Thorndike converts her into a new woman and gives to her very hardness a majesty that draws all the spirits of tragedy to her feet.[6]

Another possible model, Stanley Weintraub points out, was a man who had become in his lifetime precisely the charismatic combination of spiritual leader and undisciplined military genius that Joan of Arc had been in fifteenth-century France, namely, T. E. Lawrence (of Arabia).[7] He was a great friend of the Shaws (particularly of Charlotte), and she it was who proofread for him *The Seven Pillars of Wisdom*, a book he was working on at the same time that Shaw wrote *Saint Joan*. Consciously or not, claims Weintraub, Shaw must have been aware of the similarities between the historical and political situations in which Lawrence and his heroine found themselves: both were nationalists trying to create a unified state from a feudal order and to set a monarch upon the throne; both were successful in this enterprise, Lawrence doing for Feisel and Transjordan what Joan did for Charles VII and France; both were a nuisance to the authorities; and both preferred a primitive form of warfare and the monastic life of the barracks to love and marriage.

The final possible model for his saint is the one about whom least is known: Mary Hankinson, described by St. John Ervine as "a most likeable middle-aged woman, ... who managed summer schools for the Fabian Society, and was the sister-in-law of Francis Brett Young the novelist."[8] His authority for saying this comes from Shaw's inscription in the copy of *Saint Joan* that he gave to Mary Hankinson in 1924: "To Mary Hankinson, the only woman I know who does not believe that she was the model for Joan, and also the only woman who actually was."[9] Very little is recorded about Mary Hankinson, or "Hankie" as she was known to her friends. She was born in Cheshire into a Liberal and Victorian family, and trained at Mme Osterberg's Physical Training College in Kent.[10] She was an important member of the Fabian Society, a member of the Fabian Women's Group[11] from its foundation in 1906, and for about thirty years manager of the Fabian Summer School and captain of its cricket team.[12] She was a fine gymnast, keen on country dancing, and a strict disciplinarian. "No panky with Hanky!" was apparently the motto of the young Fabians who knew her.[13] In 1919 her spartan regime and rigid discipline in the summer school were challenged by the younger Fabians. Nevertheless, that she could inspire great affection is clear from two unpublished poems written in her honour, which have been found among the Fabian papers.

The first is an anonymous piece of doggerel called "Ode to Hanky on Her Birthday," which refers, among other things, to her flute playing, and her gym classes:

> Let all arise and her salute
> Excruciated on one boot
> And doing then the deep knee bend
> Give her our frames to rear or rend.[14]

If that does not remind us of Joan of Arc, there are stanzas in the poem which make reference, direct or indirect, to Hanky's religious outlook:

> When Hanky frowns our spirits sink
> But when she smiles the gods do wink
> We're then at Paradise's brink
> Our souls no longer are in clink.[15]

There is even a suggestion that Ethel Moor, a friend with whom Hanky shared a cottage in the Chilterns, played spiritual visitor to Hanky's Joan, in the stanza:

When Hanky calls and there is need
St. Ethel doth appear indeed
To spread her guardian angel wings
And talk of right and wrong and things.[16]

From this doggerel emerges a picture, a little blurred at the edges perhaps, of one who combined great strength of will with childlike simplicity; great honesty with great faith. The second poem, written by Shakespearean scholar John Dover Wilson in September 1911, is simply entitled "Hankie!" This clarifies the above portrait. For him she is

...the maid with silver hair
With school-boy heart and skipper air;

he too states that she

Provided soul and body food,

and stresses her strength of will and comradeship:

Like laughing skies her blue eyes glow!
Her will is firm as rocks below;
She mothers us, she helps us grow.
Who's the best comrade that we know?
Our Hanki![17]

When Mary Hankinson died in November 1952 at the age of eighty-four, an appreciation of her was published in the *Fabian News* containing a description which confirms that she could indeed, in her youth, have physically resembled Shaw's saint: "In appearance she was broad, rather short, with fair straight hair and a healthy, rather colourless complexion. She had great physical strength. I have seen three average young men, struggling unsuccessfully to get a grand piano on to a platform; she swept them aside and did it single handed."[18] At her funeral, her brother, the Rev. F. J. Hankinson, stressed her spiritual qualities: "Early in life she taught in her Sunday school, sang in the chapel choir and was always devoted to her own church, though tolerant to all creeds and races and parties."[19] He went on to describe her as a supporter of women's suffrage, as one who upheld freedom, progress, and human rights, and mentioned her sense of humour, her love of amateur theatricals, and her fondness for animals and the open air. He concluded that "Her deep faith in God showed itself in her devout and upright character and her faith in brotherhood showed itself in her selflessness and her honourable actions."[20] Small wonder, then, that Shaw admired her, or saw in her the qualities of Joan of Arc. He corresponded with her while writing *Saint Joan*, and their acquaintance continued unbroken to his death. She claimed to have memories of Shaw in Wales, Switzerland, and Keswick; only a few weeks before his fatal fall in November 1950, he sent her his latest photograph showing a frail white-bearded figure. On the back he had written: "Poor old chap! Formerly Bernard Shaw."[21]

Any one of his three friends mentioned above, it seems, could have served Shaw as a model for his heroine, and probably all did, but Shaw himself points repeatedly to a fourth figure. Time and again he stressed that, as near as possible, he had given us the real Joan of Arc in his play. To Professor Charles Sarolea he wrote:

> I do not profess to understand Joan of Arc, and neither will you, unless you are growing rasher with advancing years instead of more cautious. I took the only documents that are of the smallest value — the report of the process and that of the rehabilitation. I simply arranged what I found there for the stage, relying on Joan to pull me through, which she did.[22]

Shaw here is referring to the translation by T. Douglas Murray of J. E. J. Quicherat's *Procès de Jeanne d'Arc*. This book, presumably Cockerell's present and recommended by Leonard, was *Saint Joan*'s major source.

What other documents did Shaw consult? The earliest answer to this question was given by Bernard Shaw himself, in an interview with Archibald Henderson in the autumn of 1923, while he was still revising the proofs of *Saint Joan*, and before the play had been produced.[23] Although the records of the Roman Catholic Church regarding her canonization, according to Shaw, were not accessible, he claims to have read "all the chief sources," among them "Michelet,[24] Wallon,[25] and Martin[26] and many more; and all the reliable accounts in the encyclopaedias," including, as recorded in the original shorthand Preface, the *Encyclopaedia Britannica*. In the same interview he also admits to having seen Percy Mackaye's verse drama *Jeanne d'Arc* on the stage,[27] and exhibits easy familiarity with J. von Schiller's *Die Jungfrau von Orleans* (1801) and Mark Twain's *Personal Recollections of Joan of Arc* (1896).

The indignation that Shaw expressed in 1913 at the treatment accorded the Maid by Shakespeare and Voltaire[28] adds to the list the First Part of Shakespeare's *Henry VI* (1592), and Voltaire's *De la pucelle* (1753–56); while Andrew Lang's *The Maid of France* (1908) and Anatole France's *Vie de Jeanne d'Arc* (1910) are referred to in his Preface.

And, finally, external evidence suggests the following books as additional possible minor influences:[29] Paul de Rapin Thoyras' fifteen-volume *History of*

England (1725–31), John Speed's *Historie of Great Britaine* (1611), and Robert Southey's *Joan of Arc, an Epic Poem* (1853); these three are mentioned in an intriguing postcard to Shaw from Julius Bertram, dated 21 June 1923 (while Shaw was writing Scene V of his play): "You can have the Rapin, the Book of Days, Speed, and the Southey from here if of any use for as long as you need.... They shall be left out in case you send."

Furnished with such a wealth of information, it is hardly surprising that Shaw told Archibald Henderson, his biographer: "My Joan is more heroic and wonderful than any merely theatrical heroine ... her real attraction is that she is a fact."[30] And indeed, Shaw's play positively bristles with facts about the real Joan. In the shorthand manuscript he originally described her as

> *an ablebodied country girl of 16,*[31] *respectably dressed in red, with an uncommon face, eyes very wide apart and bulging as they often do in very imaginative people, a long well-shaped nose with wide nostrils, a short upper lip, resolute full-lipped mouth, and a handsome fighting chin.*[32] (fol. 3)

Where did Shaw discover Joan's "uncommon appearance"? Early in 1924 he had his portrait painted in oils by Walter Tittle; and, after the final sitting, spent an hour or so at the painter's studio, while waiting to rehearse *Back to Methuselah*. Conversation naturally turned to a discussion of his latest work, and, since he was talking to an artist, the physical appearance of his latest heroine. Shaw explained that the physical appearance of Joan he took from "a contemporary Gothic statue that he found in one of the French towns where much of her time was spent at the height of her success.... The natives of the place believe it to be a portrait of some saint."[33] He was here referring to the sculpted head of St. Maurice at the Musée Historique at Orleans, traditionally supposed to have been modelled from Jeanne herself when she relieved the town. Shaw may indeed have seen it there,[34] but he certainly saw the photograph of it which is the frontispiece to Murray's book.[35] Her red dress also comes from Murray, where it is mentioned no less than four times: by Jean de Metz, who claims that he saw Jeanne in Vaucouleurs "dressed in a red dress, poor and worn"; by Henri Leroyer, in whose house in that city she lodged, and who mentions a dress "of a red colour"; by Bertrand de Poulengy, who says that she put off her woman's dress "of a red colour"; and by Jean Morel of Greux, a labourer, who reports that Jeanne made him a present of a "red dress" she had been wearing. Her opening exchange with de Baudricourt is paraphrased (appropriately enough) from the 1455 deposition of Bertrand de Poulengy, who records that "She told him she came to him in the name of her Lord," and, although he does not make de Baudricourt explode in Shavian fashion in response to Jeanne's demands, but merely ask, "Who is this Lord of whom you speak?" the reply "The King of Heaven" is identical to Joan's in Shaw's play. Her next statement, that she intends to raise the siege at Orleans, is taken verbatim from Jeanne's account of the instructions she received from her voices, given to her judges on 22 February 1431 in the Castle of Rouen.

Of course, Shaw had to compress his material. As he pointed out in his "Note by the Author" in the program of the New Theatre, London, on 26 March 1924: "The visit of Joan to the Castle of Vaucouleurs, and her conquest of its captain occupy about twenty minutes on the stage. Actually she made three visits before she carried her point with him." The question which of Joan's three visits to make the subject of his first scene clearly exercised Shaw's mind. To begin with, he took the date given in Murray from the testimony of Bertrand de Poulengy: "Jeanne came to Vaucouleurs, I think, about Ascension Day [13 May 1428]."[36] Accordingly, Shaw began his play thus:

Ascension Day, 13th May, 1428, a fine spring morning. (fol. 1)

When correcting his play in Ireland, however, Shaw altered the date to 23 February 1429; an interesting alteration, and one which indicates the close attention he gave to his principal source. He had clearly decided that, rather than the first visit of Joan to Vaucouleurs, what was covered by his opening scene was the last, during which she was granted permission by de Baudricourt to go to Chinon to see the Dauphin; and from the testimony of Jean de Metz, given at Domremy in 1455 and printed in Murray, we have the date of Joan's departure from Vaucouleurs, "the first Sunday in Lent" (13 February 1429). The same witness, however, asserts that they reached Chinon after eleven days of travelling, and Murray, in a footnote, gives the date of Joan's arrival at Chinon as 6 March 1429. Accordingly, Shaw counts back eleven days and corrects not only his own stage direction, but the testimony of Jean de Metz! Later still, he was to change the opening stage direction yet again, eliminating dates altogether, and generalizing it to

A fine spring morning... in the year 1429 A.D.

Most of the remaining facts in this scene are to be found in Murray, too. Originally Shaw included, correctly, among Joan's travelling companions to Chinon, "Colet de Vienne," but he later removed him from the list, no doubt for the sake of brevity. The identification of her voices as those of Saints Catherine and Margaret comes from Jeanne's testimony on 27 February 1431; the line "They always call me Jenny in Lorraine" is from her evidence on 21 February ("In my own country they call me Jeannette"); and the idea that God

gave us our countries and our languages, and meant us to keep to them

is to be found in the letter Jeanne wrote to the King of England, the Duke of Bedford, and others, where the soldiers fighting for the King of England are told to "return to your own countries, by God's order."[37] Even Joan's casual reference to the English as "goddams" is authentic. Though it provoked one critic to deride it as "the absurdest anachronism,"[38] Shaw took it from the deposition of Raimond Sieur de Macy, who claimed that she had called them "godons"—or goddams.[39]

In view of the abundance of fact and the religious fervour of Joan herself, it is hardly surprising that so many of Shaw's friends and contemporaries thought he had turned Christian. As the painter Laurence Alma Tadema put it: "G.B.S.—do you know that your old nurse didn't sprinkle you with Holy Water for nothing? If you live to be 90 St. Joan herself will fish you up to Heaven, (she must love you and wish you were a baby)."[40] Fewer penetrated to the deeper truth, that instead of Joan converting Shaw, Shaw had subtly converted Joan to his own purposes. Proof of this is to be found not in the similarities between the events of Joan's life and Shaw's play, but in the rare but striking dissimilarities: the occasions when, unaccountably, Shaw deviates from his sources. Let us consider the first of these. In spite of Shaw's comment to Henderson that "My play is strictly historical and I shall not deviate one particle from recorded fact," there is no record, historically, of the "Miracle of the Eggs" with which the play opens. The downtrodden Steward, one remembers, is being berated by Robert de Baudricourt for announcing that there are no eggs. He attributes their absence to an act of God, and connects it with the presence of Joan, who has come to see Robert, but has been refused admittance. She manages to see him: his conversion to her scheme (to go to Chinon and see the Dauphin) is effected; and, as she leaves happily, the Steward runs in with a basket to announce that the hens are laying like mad and have produced five dozen eggs. Now according to history there was a miracle performed by Joan at Vaucouleurs, but it had to do with herrings, not chickens! She allegedly foretold the events of the Battle of Rouvray, which took place in February 1429, when a strong party of French and Scots, in attempting to cut off a convoy of men and provisions on its way from Paris to the besiegers of Orleans, was hacked to pieces and driven headlong back to Orleans. The provisions had consisted largely of salt herrings, the soldiers' main substitute for meat during Lent; and the English victors, in derision, named the day the "Battle of the Herrings." This clairvoyance—for Jeanne "avait annoncé le combat le jour même qu'il eut lieu," according to the legend—startled de Baudricourt into believing in her mission. Shaw explained, when he was asked about his omitting this, that the "Miracle of the Eggs" was substituted for the other, because the "Battle of the Herrings" would have required tedious and unnecessary explanations.[41] But the substitution gave rise to very severe criticism, particularly from the Catholics.

Christopher Hollis, for example, objected to this "miracle" not so much because of the use of hens and eggs, but because Shaw omits in his play any miracles which are not amenable to a natural explanation. He mentions in this regard the "child of Lagny"—who was dead, but was brought back to life by the prayers of

Joan and others long enough to be baptized and buried in consecrated ground: "My complaint against Mr. Shaw is not that he treats this story as a sceptic would treat it. Anatole France treated it as a sceptic would treat it, but Mr. Shaw does not treat it at all. He merely leaves it out, telling us instead about eggs."[42] And indeed, one wonders whether Shaw, in his invention of this particular occurrence, picked up a hint to be found in *Vie de Jeanne d'Arc* by Anatole France, whose sceptical remarks about the "child of Lagny" run thus: "According to the tale in circulation, during the three days since its birth the child had given no sign of life; but the gossips of Lagny had doubtless extended the period of its comatose condition, like those good wives who of a single egg laid by the husband of one of them made a hundred before the day was out."[43] But was Shaw the sceptic that France undoubtedly was when it came to Joan's miracles? Hollis thought so. So, too, does Zdeněk Vančura,[44] though he sees a dramatic use made of the scepticism: Shaw, he believes, patterns his plot in such a way that the action is suggestive of a fairy tale or a folk myth rather than of actual happenings. Vančura cites the "preposterous miracle of the eggs" as an example; the first of a regularly spaced series of dubious miracles which reduce the play to the level of a folk myth. This, he contends, is to pave the way for the really important part of the play, the discussion in the fourth act. In this he is supported by Stanley Solomon,[45] who thinks the only use of the miracles in the play is to point up Joan's pride in accepting them as a matter of course, expecting the Almighty to furnish others automatically. And Louis Crompton believes that "far from countenancing supernaturalism, Shaw treats miracles as satirically as Voltaire and France do."[46] These comments, it seems to me, are half-truths. To begin with, the miracle of the eggs is not preposterous.[47] Its most obvious source is the New Testament account of the multiplication of loaves and fishes; a miracle of Christ as valid as the raising of Lazarus—and as symbolic; for it is clearly a rehearsal of the Messianic Banquet. Moreover, importantly, it also helps to establish a peasant background for Joan, in the only scene in which she appears dressed as a woman.

But the Shavian significance of this miracle lies not in what occurs, but in when it occurs. The real Robert de Baudricourt, one remembers, was converted by Joan's clairvoyance over the "Battle of the Herrings." But although Shaw's opening scene begins with a preparation for the miracle of the eggs, and ends with its fulfilment, the real miracle at Vaucouleurs in Shaw's play concerns the power that enables a peasant maid from the marches of Lorraine to impose her superior *will* upon Squire Robert de Baudricourt without the need for conjuring tricks of any sort. For it is only *after* that miracle has been accomplished, and Joan is on her way to Chinon, that the Steward enters, tardily, to report the accomplishments of the hens! In fact the prime function of the Steward in the first part of this scene is to emphasize the difficulty of the task confronting Joan by revealing de Baudricourt's own strength, both of will and of body; and this he does by being systematically bullied and beaten until the entrance of the Maid.[48] Shaw, then, is illustrating the belief of de Poulengy in that scene when, in response to de Baudricourt's sneer, "Oh, you think the girl can work miracles, do you?" he replies, "I think the girl herself is a bit of a miracle."

Bertrand de Poulengy, a young squire who later accompanied Joan to Chinon, is the last character to enter in Scene I. Warrant for his presence at the interview between Joan and de Baudricourt is contained in his 1455 deposition, given at Domremy ("I saw her speaking to the Captain, Robert de Baudricourt"),[49] from which Shaw had already taken some of Joan's dialogue. Shaw's description of Bertrand de Poulengy was also perhaps inspired by an illustration in Murray:

> a young French gentleman-at-arms, a year or two younger than Robert, wearing his hair longer, a warrior with a touch of the troubadour which gives him some poetic beauty. (fol. 4)

In revision, however, the word "young" was replaced by "lymphatic," and the "warrior," and "troubadour" references were removed for the character to provide a better contrast to the volatile and self-assertive de Baudricourt.

Shaw's Act I, as it was originally called, was finished at Stratford-on-Avon. Possibly Shakespeare's birthplace made him think in acts instead of scenes; certainly, Scene II, as it is now, was originally called Act II when it was started at Ayot in May 1923. At that time, Shaw was in correspondence with his friend William Archer concerning the staging of Shakespeare's plays. Shaw was of the opinion that the realism of externals "consummated" and symbolized in the box room was exploded. In Archer's letter to Shaw, dated 12 June 1923, his old friend and critic disagreed, although he conceded that the attempt to apply "box room principles" to Shakespeare was "foolish and futile," concluding that certain gifted directors (he names Barker and Bridges Adams) had arrived at an "excellent compromise between the pictorial and the platform stage." And he adds: "You do well to adopt it for Joan of Arc. But if you apply it to securing a non-stop performance you go utterly wrong. The act was a great invention of the Greeks, and no great dramatist has ever ignored it."[50]

The scene in which Joan meets the Dauphin to tell him of her mission is thoroughly treated by most of Shaw's sources: its pattern, and even the characters who took part in it, well established. In Murray, from the testimony of Dunois given in 1455, Shaw read that, after his meeting with her, the Dauphin sent Joan with the Lord Archbishop of Rheims, then chancellor of France, to Blois, where those were who had the charge of escorting her convoy, including the Sieur de Rais (Gilles de Laval, otherwise known as Bluebeard),[51] de Boussac, Marshal of France, de Coulent, Admiral of France, La Hire, and Ambroise de Loré who was afterwards governor of Paris. Mark Twain's *Personal Recollections of Joan of Arc*

(1896) which, as we have seen, Shaw was familiar with,[52] tells us that three or four of the King's counsellors were always nearest his person,

> schemers and traitors everyone — that put obstructions in the way, and seek always, by lies and pretexts, to make delay. Chiefest of these are Georges de la Trémouille and that plotting fox the Archbishop of Rheims.[53]

And these two are, if not plotting, at least in conversation about the King at the commencement of Shaw's second scene.

It is Anatole France who supplies the text for that conversation by pointing out that, although the only title carried by La Trémouille was that of *conceiller-chambellan*, he was also the Grand Usurer of the Kingdom, his debtors being "the king, and a multitude of nobles, high and low."[54] Their duologue serves to reveal their characters and also the King's poverty, both of money and of courage. Mark Twain had also stressed this:

> It is a marvel that any man in such desperate case as is the king can moon around in his torpid way, and see his all go to ruin without lifting a finger to stay the disaster. What a most strange spectacle it is! Here he is shut up in this wee corner of the realm like a rat in a trap;[55] his royal shelter this huge gloomy tomb of a castle, with wormy rags for upholstery and crippled furniture for use, a very house of desolation; in his treasury forty francs, and not a farthing more, God be witness! no army, nor any shadow of one; and by contrast with this hungry poverty you behold this crownless pauper and his shoals of fools and favourites tricked out in the gaudiest silks and velvets you shall find in any Court in Christendom.[56]

The conversation of La Trémouille and the Archbishop is interrupted by the arrival of a page, who announces Bluebeard and La Hire with the words "Something has happened." The happening in question is taken from Murray, specifically the Paris deposition of Brother Jean Pasquerel, who relates:

> The day on which this interview [between Joan and the Dauphin] was to take place, just as she entered the castle, a man, mounted on horseback, said, "Is that the Maid?" He insulted her, and swore with horrid blasphemy. "Oh! In God's name," she said to him, "Dost thou blaspheme God, thou who art so near thy death!" And, an hour after, this man fell into the water and was drowned. I report this fact as I gathered it from Jeanne and from many others who said they had been witnesses of it.[57]

Shaw uses the report of this incident in a semi-humorous fashion to help pave the way for the arrival of the Maid, and to establish the character of La Hire. Shaw's picture of this bluff, blaspheming, but fundamentally friendly soldier may have been inspired by any of his sources. Certainly, at this point in his play, literary memories may have come back to him. Percy Mackaye's *Jeanne d'Arc*, which Shaw had seen in May 1907, contains many of the same characters as *Saint Joan*. Apart from Jeanne and Charles VII, it also presents the persons of La Trémouille (described as Charles's favourite), the Archbishop of Rheims, Dunois, and La Hire. Moreover, its second act is, like Shaw's, set in the Castle of Chinon on 8 March 1429.[58] Mackaye's La Hire, in particular, is reminiscent of Shaw's creation. He is the same hotheaded and exclamatory character, intemperate of language but fierce in defence of the Maid. When La Trémouille in *Jeanne d'Arc* makes a scurrilous remark about Joan, La Hire explodes:

> Tonerre de dieu! What man hath seen the face
> Of Jeanne the Maid and named her charlatan?
> Her face—God's eyes! when I am cooked and damn'd,
> And devils twirl me on a spit in hell,
> I'll think upon that face and have redemption.[59]

Joan's "miracle" in Scene II, namely, the discovery of the real Dauphin, when someone had taken his place on the throne seat, is a tradition rooted in fact. Indeed, there seems a possibility that the test was deliberately set up at Joan's own behest. Jeanne d'Arc's testimony, given on 27 February 1431 and quoted in Murray, contains the following:

> Afterwards, I went to the Castle of Chinon, whence I sent letters to the king, to know if I should be allowed to see him; saying, that I had travelled a hundred and fifty leagues to come to his help, and that I knew many things good for him. *I think I remember there was in my letter the remark that I should recognize him among all others.*[60]

Her recognition of the Dauphin in Shaw's play is important from the standpoint of the Dauphin himself; for, according to Shaw, it would convince him that he was of the blood royal. Some say that the "secret" the real Jeanne is supposed to have told Charles privately, was that she knew of his fears in this regard, and even his most intimate prayers about it. Be that as it may, all fictional treatments of the story have stressed this "miracle." In Southey's epic poem, *Joan of Arc*, for example, the Dauphin suggests that he should hide among his courtiers:

> On the throne meantime,
> I the while mingling with the menial throng,
> Some courtier shall be seated. If this Maid

Be by the Holy Spirit of God inspir'd,
That Holy Spirit will gift her with the power
To pierce deception. But if strange of mind
Enthusiast fancy fire her wilder'd brain,
Thus proved, she to obscurity again
May guiltlessly retire.[61]

Subsequently, the Maid recognizes the Dauphin, and thus Southey indicates that
she was inspired by the Holy Spirit. Perhaps nothing stresses more vividly the
difference between Shaw and his predecessors, in their treatment of the Joan of
Arc story, than a comparison between Percy Mackaye's *Jeanne d'Arc* and Shaw's
Saint Joan at this moment. In *Jeanne d'Arc*, the heroine hesitates in the dark hall,
trying to locate the king, while the eyes of all are centred upon her:

> there emerges from the great fireplace, where logs are burning, and stands
> upon the hearth with flaming wings, St. Michael, who gazes also at Jeanne.
> The only sound or other motion in the hall is caused by the Court-fool, who
> springing up from the throne-footstool to whisper of the Maid in d'Alen-
> çon's ear, sets thereby the bells on his cap to tinkling silverly. Simul-
> taneously, the voice of St. Catherine speaks, as from mid-air:
>
> VOICE: Daughter of God, choose boldly.
>
> Glancing slowly through the hall, the eyes of Jeanne meet those of St.
> Michael who points with his hand at Charles, then turns and disappears
> within the smoke and glow of the fireplace.[62]

Shaw is much more pragmatic about her success.[63] It is again the Dauphin in
Saint Joan who decides that someone shall substitute for him. And he chooses
Bluebeard:

> Come with me, Bluebeard; and let us arrange so that she may not know who
> I am. You will pretend to be me. (fol. 14)

The Archbishop, appropriately enough for Shaw's purposes, is the one in *Saint
Joan* who declares that the Maid will have no difficulty distinguishing between
the two. La Trémouille is surprised:

> Why, How is she to know?
> The Archbishop = She will know that the Dauphin is the meanest looking and
> worst dressed figure in the Court. She will know his age. (fol. 14)

This idea was not Shaw's. He probably obtained it from Anatole France, who says:

> Afterwards there were those who marvelled that she should have recognized him in the midst of nobles more magnificently dressed than he. It is possible that on that day he may have been poorly attired. We know that it was his custom to have new sleeves put to his old doublets. And in any case he did not show off his clothes. Very ugly, knock-kneed, with emaciated thighs, small, odd, blinking eyes, and a large bulbous nose, on his bony, bandy legs tottered and trembled this prince of twenty-six.[64]

Andrew Lang in 1908 repeats the idea: "She had recognized Charles at once, and it is certain that in her opinion, she did so spontaneously. He is said to have been an ugly young man, as we saw, with legs like those of our own James VI." There were, however, two traditions about Charles's appearance. Some saw him as Shaw describes him,

> *a poor creature physically; and the current fashion of shaving closely and hiding every scrap of hair under the headcovering or headdress, both by women and men makes the very worst of his appearance. He has little narrow eyes, close together, a long pendulous nose that droops over his thick short upper lip, and the expression of a dog accustomed to be kicked and hopeless of any better treatment. This, and his small ricketty figure and spindle shanks, give a certain pathos to the mockery of his exalted position.* (fol. 11)

This description, modified somewhat later by the removal of the reference to "spindle shanks," represents one tradition; and caused complaints from early audiences. The reviewer in the *Theatre Magazine*, in March 1924, was annoyed: "It is not...clear why the descendant of St. Louis is presented as a semi-imbecile, repellent in face and manner. This is taking unwarranted liberties with history."[65]

And indeed, according to the second tradition, he was good-looking. "He was, in person, a handsome prince, and handsome in speech with all persons," reports his contemporary Monstrelet. But ideas of beauty change; and Shaw had in front of him, in Murray, a reproduction of the painting of Charles VII from the Louvre, which is certainly not the portrait of a handsome man by twentieth-century standards, and of which his introductory stage direction, quoted above, could be a fairly objective description.

So far as his personality is concerned, even Monstrelet agrees that "he did not readily put on his harness, and he had no heart for war if he could do without it." Not only does Shaw stress this several times, making his courtiers taunt the

Dauphin with his cowardice, but in the original manuscript, before correction, in the subsequent scene between Joan and Charles when the court has left, so profound is the Dauphin's distaste for any form of warfare that he actually blunts Joan's purpose in coming to crown him!

In this version, Charles confesses his fear to Joan, and she vows she will put courage into him. She remarks on his poor dress, and Charles says he does not look good in clothes anyway. The dialogue continues thus:

Joan = There is some good in thee, Charlie; but it is not a king's good.

Charles = We shall see. I have my eyes open; and I can tell you that one good treaty is worth ten good fights. These fighting fellows lose all on the treaties that they gain on the fights. They go into battle swearing that they will either die or win this or that; but in the end what they win is neither this nor that, but always the other. The losers are often none the worse; and the winners always have their heads broken. So I tell you once for all, if the English capture you at Orleans I wont fight for you, because I cant; and I wont ransom you, because I have no money; when it comes to a treaty the English are sure to have the worst of it because they understand nothing but fighting.

Joan [with sudden anguish] Gentle Dauphin: I came to give you courage; and now you have taken away mine. The world has gone grey for me. [She falls on her knees and clasps her hands]. Blessed Margaret, blessed Catherine, holy Michael: I am in trouble. Help me and counsel me. (fol. 18)

At this point Charles complains petulantly about her praying (as he does in the final version), and finally, after more argument, much of which is also retained, Joan, speaking of his kingdom, says:

And you have sold it all for a mess of pottage. Your grandfather was Charles the Wise: you will not even be Charles the Damned: Damnation is too dignified for you.

Charles = Yes: bully me: talk me down. Everybody bullies me: everybody talks me down. But I have my own opinion still.

Joan = I shall go back to the farm and wait for my death. This world is no place for me.

Charles = No: dont do that: dont be unreasonable. I want you to stay.

Joan = What for?

Charles = To keep up the miracle, of course.

Joan = What miracle?

Charles = Your picking me out as the royal king of France.

Joan [a mirthless little laugh]!

Charles [continuing] That showed that I was really of the blood royal. You know my mother denies it. You dont know how much good you have done me by that miracle. Dont go back on me now. I will give you soldiers to go to Orleans. I will give you money—as much as like (sic)—as soon as I can borrow it. Dont be unkind. Please.

Joan = I must save Orleans. I must save France. I must have thee crowned and pretend thou art a true king, and for that lie I shall be betrayed by thee, thou poor little Judas.

Charles = If only you would do it without bullying me! (fols. 19, 20)

And that is how the original Act II ended. One can only guess at what point Shaw changed the ending to the one we now have; but one fancies that it would be an early alteration. For the original was in the wrong key. It was too soon for Joan to become discouraged. It was awkward to have her calling onstage for angelic help (although Percy Mackaye hadn't hesitated to have her do so); and Shaw had not been able to construct a reply to her plea. Her talk about going back to the farm and Charles's statements about not being able to ransom her were saved up to be used in Scene V when the key of the play changes. But in Scene II the action is still a rising one; and so the speeches were all deleted, and the present ending appended. Nevertheless, they do point to the desire that Shaw clearly has to establish Charles in the audience's mind as a person strikingly unkinglike; and this suggests a dramatic reason for his choice of the Charles VII tradition that represents the Dauphin as ugly and cowardly. For had Charles been anything like a king to begin with, Joan's task would have been easy. As it is, with Shaw's Dauphin, it becomes one of the labours of Hercules. In other words, Scene II presents an interesting parallel to Scene I. In the opening scene, as I have pointed out, there was an ostensible miracle, the mass production of eggs and milk; and a real miracle, the conversion of de Baudricourt from sceptic to believer. Similarly, in Scene II, we are presented with an apparent miracle, which satisfies the dramatis personae, namely, the discovery of the rightful king among the courtiers; but also a real miracle in the transformation of that most unsuitable, weak-willed personage into an embryonic leader. Accordingly, in the light of this "miracle" Shaw required a more triumphant ending to his scene, and decided to bring the rest of the court back onto the stage, make Charles demonstrate his new-found courage by giving charge of the army to Joan, and conclude with the Knights and La Hire all shouting for the Maid. Perhaps this revised ending was again suggested by Mark Twain's *Personal Recollections of Joan of Arc*. In that book, when the Dauphin gives charge of the army to the Maid, a herald proclaims:

"Know all men, and take heed therefore, that the most high, the most illustrious Charles, by the Grace of God King of France, hath been pleased to confer upon his well-beloved servant Joan of Arc, called the Maid, the title, emoluments, authorities, and dignity of General-in-Chief of the armies of France." Here a thousand caps flew into the air and the multitude burst into a hurricane of cheers that raged till it seemed as if it would never come to an end.[66]

The rising action of the play climaxes in its briefest, yet perhaps most beautiful, scene, Scene III,[67] set on the banks of the River Loire. Originally, Shaw was most specific, using facts from the Duc D'Alençon's testimony in Murray to place it "on the patch of ground between the church of St. Jean de Loup and the river"; later he generalized it to "a patch of ground on the south bank of the silver Loire." Shaw's description of the scene bears an interesting resemblance to the description given by Mrs. Florence Caddy, who speaks of the River Meuse

> sparkling like a silver riband with fringed edges. . . . kingfishers haunt these waters and gleam like sapphires among the sedges.[68]

Kingfishers inhabit Shaw's Loire, too; Dunois' Page spots one and they watch it eagerly until it takes cover. The incident, however trivial it might appear, is probably drawn from fact. In a letter to Shaw, Sir Sydney Cockerell claims, "I was the boy who pointed to the kingfisher at Chateau Gaillard (transferred to the Loire)."[69] Nor is the incident so trivial. The Virgin Mary, Dunois reminds us, wore a hood "kingfisher colour"; he awaits a virgin; and the Page, admiring the flight of the birds, says:

> Arnt they lovely? I wish I could catch them.
> Dunois = Let me catch *you* trying to trap them, and I will put you into the iron cage for the (*sic*) month to teach you what a cage feels like. (fol. 21)

It is the first reference in the play to imprisonment. Hideo Takeuchi makes the suggestion that Shaw covered deficiencies in his verbal poetry by such romantic settings as the Loire scene.[70] We shall return to this comment later. Perhaps deficiencies in Dunois' verbal poetry appear as he paces the riverbank, apostrophizing the west wind, but they are in keeping with his character as Shaw presents him, the practical soldier. His physical appearance almost certainly derives from the engraving in Murray:

> *His broad brow and pointed chin give him an equilaterally triangular face.* (fol. 21)

This appearance, in the picture, is accentuated by his tricorn hat which, apart from its plume, looks like that of an admiral. Certainly, too, Dunois' face in the illustration could be described as having "the expression of a good-natured and capable man who has no affectations and no foolish illusions." He is riding a horse and carries his shield which bears his coat of arms. An alteration in Shaw's play may have been suggested by that. In reply to Joan's "Be you Bastard of Orleans?" Dunois had originally replied, "I am."[71] Later this was altered to "You see the bend sinister." Certainly this is what Shaw had seen in the Murray illustration of Dunois holding his shield. Shaw had also studied carefully Dunois' own deposition given at Orleans in 1455, for he uses many of Dunois' actual expressions. In the "Note by the Author" from the program of the New Theatre, London, 26 March 1924, Shaw says: "It has been assumed that the military conversation of Dunois may safely be founded on that of his colleague the Duc d'Alençon, who does not appear in the play." This is more true of the Dunois of Scene V, but perhaps it also points to a rather interesting difference between the character of Dunois in Murray and that of Dunois in Shaw's play. The opening of Dunois' testimony at Orleans in Murray is

> I think that Jeanne was sent by God.[72]

—a line which Shaw does give to Dunois in the later scene; but it is a repeated thought in the real Dunois' testimony, in which he gives several lengthy reasons for believing such a thing. Inevitably, in so doing, he plays down his own military ability, giving great credit to the Maid. Perhaps as a consequence, all sources, factual and fictional, stress Joan's power at the Siege of Orleans. However, in Scene III, Shaw makes Dunois her teacher. He is not a person as weak-willed as de Baudricourt or Charles. He is the first man in the play whose lines have the Shavian ring of authority. On one occasion he resembles Bluntschli in *Arms and the Man*, and Joan finds herself treated like Raina, when she pleads with him:

> Oh, why are you not fighting? Listen to me: I will deliver you from fear. I—
> Dunois [laughing heartily and waving her off] No no, my girl: if you delivered me from fear I should be a good knight for a story book, but a very bad commander for the army. Come: let me begin to make a soldier of you. (fol. 22)

This impression of Dunois' authority is reinforced by the omission, in the final version, of the following brief dispute over tactics, which Joan wins!

> Dunois = ...It is for God we are waiting. We cannot take those forts by a sally across the bridge. I must launch an attack by water and take the English in the rear. And you must take your troops down the river to Blois and cross the bridge there. You will come back along the south bank and wait until my troops come across by boat to you. I will arrange that you and they shall fall on the English together at the right moment.

Joan = But there is no sense in it: you will drive them across the bridge into the town instead of away from it.

Dunois = They shall have a warm welcome: I will answer for that.

Joan = But how far is Blois?

Dunois = Twelve leagues.

Joan = Twelve leagues. Twenty four leagues there and back. Two days—three days march, and our men dog tired at the end of it! You are crazy. I will not have it so. Make your men embark at once. Let them make rafts and put big guns on them and make the English afraid to go out of their trenches. I will attack by the bridge and take the forts. (fol. 23)

Of course, another reason for the excision of the above is that, however factually based it may be, it is too complicated, and slows the movement of the scene.[73] But without it Dunois retains his stature as a general and as a man not easily impressed or outfaced, even by Joan of Arc. It will take a genuine miracle to convince him.

Accordingly, Shaw provides one. And, at this point, I want to return to the comment made by Hideo Takeuchi: that Shaw's setting covered deficiencies in his poetry. The fact is that the setting and the verbal poetry create a fitting atmosphere for a miracle which would have less dramatic impact without them. The miracle itself is very simply presented: the pennon flying from Dunois' lance in the east breeze reverses itself and streams westward. But the change of wind, which is natural, and which occurs, one notices, before Joan can go to church to pray for it, is, unlike the earlier miracles, "accepted" both by the characters on stage and by the audience as the revealed hand of God. This is in large part due to the emotion generated during the scene by the setting, by Dunois' broken attempts at verse, by the excitement over the kingfishers, and by the comradely relationship struck between the saint and the soldier. Indeed, the latter's avuncular amusement at Joan's headstrong fighting instinct and her lack of tactics leads to the emotion-charged moment when Dunois kneels and presents his baton to the Maid, saying:

God has spoken. You are our commander of the king's army;

just as it makes possible Joan's beautiful speech:

Dunois, dear comrade in arms, help me. My eyes are blinded with tears. Set my foot on the bridge, and say "Go forward." (fols. 23, 23v)

And Dunois' final roar of triumph, added during revision:

Never mind the tears: make for the flash of the guns.

3

The Cunning Counsellors

Shaw seems to have hesitated momentarily when beginning Scene IV.[1] Originally he intended to introduce three new characters, and began:

> Talbot, Glassdale and the Earl of Warwick seated at a table looking very glum.[2]

But after only two lines of dialogue, Talbot was dismissed:

> Talbot = Nice news, by heaven, to send a strumpet after England!
> Warwick = The damned witch. If I catch her I will brain the sorcery out of her.
> Talbot = Thank God I was not beaten by a man.

The above shorthand was deleted, and a setting established:

> A room in the inn. The Earl of Warwick, aged ---, seated at the table reading dispatches. Besides papers a Book of Hours lies within his reach. (fol. 24)

This, too, was scratched out, and finally the setting and characters as they now stand were introduced: a tent in the English camp, containing the Earl of Warwick and his foil, the chaplain John de Stogumber.

Although the age of the former is given in the final version as fifty, the text indicates that the scene takes place during one of the Earl's infrequent trips to France (he was Captain of Calais) in 1428, at which time he was forty-six years old.[3] One critic complains that this historical inaccuracy makes it appear as if Warwick were already planning the condemnation of Joan in the summer of 1429.[4] But Shaw deliberately fashioned his Earl of Warwick to emphasize his part in Joan's downfall. In a portion of the original shorthand Preface, subsequently discarded, he had complained of the removal of the Earl's responsibility for this in the official accounts:

Only in Warwick's case is the paper fairly blank: for our courtly Encyclopaedia Britannica, in its highly appreciative article on him, says not one word of his share in the disposal of Joan, which was by far the most memorable event in his life. Only in England could an earl depend on such delicate consideration five hundred years after his death. (fol. 96)

Taking issue with the manner rather than the matter, Desmond MacCarthy points out that the Earl is not a Renaissance man at all, but is a "purely eighteenth century nobleman," likening him to Burgoyne in *The Devil's Disciple*, and his clerical secretary, de Stogumber, to Britannus in *Caesar and Cleopatra*.[5] And de Stogumber is avowedly a Shavian invention, drawn from a mere hint in Murray, where, according to Shaw, he is known only by his having lost his temper and called Cauchon a traitor for accepting Joan's recantation.[6] However, in making de Stogumber Keeper of the Private Seal to the Cardinal of Winchester, Shaw is making a historical point and seeking to establish an attitude. Henry Beaufort, the Cardinal of Winchester, uncle to both the Protector Gloucester and Bedford, had become extremely powerful in England during the French War. He had progressively reduced the Protector's influence, and desired to bring Bedford, struggling unsuccessfully in France, as low as Gloucester in England, that his own power might be greater yet. He already had an army in readiness with which ostensibly he had been going to suppress the Bohemian Hussites; but yielding to the pleadings of Bedford, he took it to France instead, and entered Paris with his army on 25 July 1429. Later, desiring to have his great nephew Henry VI anointed in Paris, Winchester set about discrediting Charles VII's coronation by claiming that Joan was a witch: it therefore followed that her victories in the field were the result of sorcery; and it was largely at Winchester's instigation that Joan was tried for witchcraft. The attitude Shaw gives to de Stogumber clearly derives from Winchester's frame of mind: it is a confusion of superstition, patriotism, and power seeking. Shaw in the note above also records that de Stogumber's "Devonshire name was borrowed for the occasion."

The Tent Scene, as critics call it, is extraordinarily effective from the dramatic standpoint. In Warwick and de Stogumber, Shaw is presenting, as he did in the case of Burgoyne and Swindon, the two types of Englishmen in whom he most delighted: the clear-sighted cynic, who sees through the system to the inevitable human frailty behind it, yet who uses it for his own ends, and the emotional patriot and true believer in all the sham ideals that bolster his love of king and country. In the Tent Scene, the additional presence of a French prelate is an ironic bonus, revealing, as it does, both the national differences and the psychological similarities of the three men. Shaw's portrait of Cauchon has been the cause of some critical disapproval. In the Preface he confesses that he has flattered Cauchon nearly as much as the melodramatist has vilified him, in a search for the "innermost attainable truth"; and this statement to some extent takes the sting out of such criticisms as those of Christopher Hollis, who complains about Shaw's admiration of Cauchon. But this confession has not placated all critics, and recently a whole article has been devoted to the "Shavianization" of Cauchon, in which the author, M. A. Cohen, claims that Cauchon is flattered in the interests of a characteristically Shavian tragic moral—the tragedy of murders not committed by murderers, but by "normally innocent people in the energy of their righteousness." He concedes that there is value in this point, which "alerts us to the fact that the persecution and murder of innocents may be done by 'normal' persons, perhaps a bit like ourselves"; but states nevertheless that the historical instance is wrong because "Cauchon and his associates were obvious knaves."[7] The obviousness of Cauchon's knavery, however, as Cohen himself agrees, is not to be deduced from new facts discovered about him; it is upon the interpretation of the old facts. And here appears the fundamental weakness of his argument. The facts are plentiful: Cauchon had been forced to flee from both Rheims and Beauvais during the absence of Charles's troops. Far from being "no political bishop" as he claims, he was a principal supporter of the "double monarchy" theory which advocated that Burgundy and the Armagnac regions of France should be separate kingdoms under English overlordship. He offered thousands of francs for the handing over of Joan to the Church. In this he acted with the complete support of the strongly pro-English University of Paris, which also backed him as judge for the trial, even though he had no authority to hold such office in Rouen.[8]

In the above account the facts are plentiful; it is the motives that are missing. Shaw has supplied Cauchon with one set of motives; M. A. Cohen has supplied him with another. There is nothing in the facts to suggest that Pierre Cauchon was not a devoutly religious man. That he should have held political opinions at such a time was only to be expected, and is demonstrated by Shaw in the Tent Scene, where, incidentally, his anger at Warwick's assumption that he should cheerfully put his religion aside, prompts the line, "I am no *mere* political bishop"—the adverb modifying the sense importantly. That he should have "offered thousands" for Joan to be handed over to the Church is perfectly consistent with his belief that she was a heretic (a belief also expounded in the Tent Scene), and even if we accept the implication that he wished to be the judge at the trial, to assume that he wished to be so for dishonourable rather than honourable motives is a mere assumption.

In short, a reading of M. A. Cohen's article does not convince me that he is closer to the truth about Cauchon than was Shaw. The motives he imputes to Cauchon are in any case derived largely from the "leading modern authority," Régine Pernoud, a writer who, Cohen agrees, makes a more "sweeping indictment of the trial" than others have. And that we are not in the realm of fact but speculation is clear from the use he makes of her book: "*Pernoud suggests* that the actual Cauchon made the masculine clothes the main issue. . . . *In her view*, Cauchon made the wearing of the clothes the symbol of Joan's failure to submit to the Church. . . . *Pernoud feels* that Cauchon rode roughshod over the majority of the assessors."[9] In short, the Cauchon presented to us by M. A. Cohen has been "Pernoudized" quite as much as the character in the play has been "Shavianized"; and one is tempted to say that the process of "villainizing" this man has probably been collectively carried on for centuries by those who, for the most obvious human reasons, would prefer to be as unlike Peter Cauchon as possible.

The Tent Scene is, as Reginald Owen said in his December 1924 review in the *Drama*, Shaw at his best. The Earl of Warwick, the Chaplain de Stogumber, and the Bishop of Beauvais debate what shall be done to the Maid, while Shaw expresses his own convictions about heresy and orthodoxy, about church, state, and individual in a way that draws the middle ages and the twentieth century close together. He also demonstrates the culmination of a technique he had practised all his writing life; a technique he had admired in Ibsen:

> nor does the villain forge or assassinate, since he is a villain by virtue of his determination to do nothing wrong.[10]

Shaw's "villains," too, are determined "to do no wrong," and from Sartorius to Cauchon are masters of self-justification. The trio in the Tent Scene exhibit the Shavian technique to perfection, in spite of the challenge; for it is not easy to rationalize one's desire to burn a seventeen-year-old girl. The impact of the scene derives in large part from the tension set up between our admiration of the speakers' logic, and our abhorrence at their conclusion.

Arthur Mizener, in a lecture to the English Institute on "Poetic Drama and the Well-Made Play," praised the conclusion of the Tent Scene:

> The scene ends with Warwick's rising, politely but authoritatively. "My Lord," he says to Cauchon, "we seem to be agreed."
>
> CAUCHON [rising also, but in protest] I will not imperil my soul. I will uphold the justice of the Church. I will strive to the utmost for this woman's salvation.
> WARWICK. I am sorry for the poor girl. I hate these severities. I will spare her if I can.
> THE CHAPLAIN [implacably] I would burn her with my own hands.
> CAUCHON [blessing him] Sancta simplicitas!
>
> And the curtain descends on the tableau. It is a magnificent though entirely conventional moment—perhaps I ought properly to say, *because* entirely conventional. Without stepping outside the habitual language of its theatre,

it even gets most of the advantages of verse. Cauchon and Warwick each speak three declarative sentences which are parallel in structure and three-stressed. De Stogumber caps their exchange with one more such sentence and Cauchon rounds off the pattern with his comment, which—counting the necessary pause before it—is also three-stressed.[11]

The comment on the poetic rhythm is perceptive, for originally Shaw had finished the scene with the Chaplain's barely controlled angry remark. During his revision in Ireland he added Cauchon's blessing partly to complete the cadence, and partly because the Bishop's gesture applies not only to de Stogumber: it is a chillingly ironic comment on the whole scene. Indeed, the irony deepens when one realizes that the Bishop's final remark is a grim echo of the last words of John Huss, who, about to be burnt at the stake for heresy, was moved to exclaim "O sancta simplicitas!" (Oh holy simplicity!) when he saw an old peasant bringing a faggot to throw on the pile![12]

Most corrected of all the scenes in the original manuscript, Scene V finally contains some of the finest writing of the whole play.[13] Shaw's problem, judging by the deletions, was principally the one mentioned by Helen MacAfee in the *Yale Review*, January 1925: "With most historical pieces, the dramatist's problem is to keep the facts from running away with the structure and falling into a mere animated chronicle." The problem was particularly acute for Shaw in *Saint Joan*, because he wished to *insist* on the facts, and dismiss the romantic fictions which clung to his warrior-saint; and he also wanted to suggest her qualities of leadership without resorting to a stage attempt to depict the French army.[14]

Again, Shaw's principal source for the scene was Murray, who may, indeed, have given him the idea for it. It is Murray who speaks of the "waning of [Joan's] powers after the coronation of Rheims,"[15] reminding us that Shaw's play is divided into three scenes of rising action in which Joan is seen victorious, a scene in which she is absent but in which her fate is decided upon, and three scenes of falling action in which she is seen defeated: once by those she believed her friends, once by her enemies, and finally by the world. This, then, the coronation, marks the beginning of that decline; and as Murray says,

> her appeal to Charles after the coronation to be allowed to return to her father and mother, supported by contemporary authority, seems to show that she looked upon her work as done, and the great outburst of weeping in the Cathedral was in all likelihood the sob of satisfied piety and patriotism, whose cares were at an end and whose task was fulfilled even to fruition.[16]

Shortly after this moment Shaw's scene begins, an addition in the printed version of the play in Ireland being the lengthening of Dunois' sentence, "You will catch a chill if you stay here any longer," which becomes, "*After that fit of crying*, you will catch a chill if you stay here any longer." But in its original state, the scene contained much more military fact; and, as in the original draft of Scene III, Dunois was still Joan's teacher:

> Let me give you a piece of advice, as I shall not always be at your side in battle. Never let yourself stray so far from your staff that you can be cut off from them. Do not be the last to retire when the retirement is across a drawbridge. Those who are safely inside may drop the portcullis in front of your nose, and receive a share of your ransom for their pains. Many a good man has been sold that way.[17] (fol. 34)

In fact, Joan herself, in this first version of the scene, seems determined to destroy the image of herself as a warrior-saint:

Joan = I know very well that you and the other nobles do not consider me a soldier. You try to keep me out of the vanguard. You tell me nothing of your plans. You carry me about as a mascot, just good enough to encourage the soldiers and frighten the English. As if I could not see through you!

Dunois = We do not want to have you killed, Joan. Where should we be without the Maid and her white banner?

Joan = It is all lies.

Dunois = It was not all lies when you took the Boulevard at Orleans, Joan.

Joan = Yes it was. Why do you give me the credit that is due to poor d'Aulon and the brave Basque? I had not my banner at all. It was d'Aulon who had it. He gave it to the Basque and made the Basque promise to follow him. Then he went right down into the moat and up to the wall with his shield over his head: the goddams were raining stones down on him. And the Basque was following him when I saw him with my banner and lost my head like a silly goose and began screaming "My banner, my banner" and tried to tear it away out of his hand. D'Aulon called out "Is that how you keep your promise, Basque"; and then the Basque just sent me flying and charged into the moat with nothing but the banner to keep the stones off him. Next moment we were all over the English. Why do you give me the credit when it is really due to d'Aulon and the Basque?

Dunois = It produces a better effect to give the credit to the Maid and make a miracle of it.

Joan = But it isnt fair to d'Aulon.

Dunois [coolly] In war the young do the work and the commanders get the credit. But when the young grow old they get the credit and the young do the work. So never fear: d'Aulon's turn will come. (fol. 35)

The facts of this passage, removed in its entirety from the printed version, Shaw adapted from the 1456 testimony of Jeanne's Steward, d'Aulon, to be found on pages 316–17 of Murray's book.[18] It is a vivid account, all the more exciting for the matter-of-fact soldierly tone adopted by d'Aulon, whom Shaw follows very closely. While its deletion decreases our awareness of the wars in which Joan was engaged, the traditional view of Joan the military genius is preserved; and this view, though objected to most vehemently by J. M. Robertson in his book *Mr. Shaw and "The Maid,"* is adequately supported by the evidence of the Duc d'Alençon.

Another aspect of Scene V which assists in creating the tragic atmosphere is the heightening of language. At least one alteration in revision entailed the reduction of inadequate poetry. At the beginning of the scene, in her conversation with Dunois, Joan complains that she finds the quietness after the battle dull, "where we are like the leaden soldiers that children play with: only a show. I care for nothing but the real thing. The real thing, eh Dunois?" These lines were removed in revision; but during this process other poetic touches were added, as, for example, when Joan is speaking to La Hire a little later in the scene. Originally the dialogue read:

> La Hire: in spite of all your sins we shall meet in heaven; for I love you as I love Pitou my old sheepdog [They all laugh except La Hire who nods understandingly].
> Joan [continuing] Pitou can kill a wolf. You will kill the English wolves until they go back to their country and become good dogs of God, will you not? (fol. 36)

La Hire's original reply ran:

> I will do my best by them.

In the first revisions, carried out in Ireland, La Hire is made to reply instead:

> You and I together: yes.

This prompts Joan's dramatic response, not found in the first manuscript:

> No: I shall last only a year from the beginning.
> ALL THE OTHERS. What!
> JOAN. I know it somehow.
> DUNOIS. Nonsense!

This idea originates in the Duc d'Alençon's testimony. He reports:

> Many times in my presence Jeanne told the king she would last but one year
> and no more; and that she should consider how best to employ this year.[19]

And Mark Twain had also seen the dramatic potential of such a remark:

> After a moment she spoke out with what seemed a sort of terrified impulse,
> and said "Oh use me; I beseech you use me—there is but little time!"
> "But little time?"
> "Only a year—I shall last only a year."[20]

Elsewhere, too, in this scene, some revisions, particularly of Joan's speeches, seem
designed to enhance poetic effect:

British Library Add. MSS. 45923, fol. 34	*Saint Joan* (London: Constable & Co., 1924)
General: the world is too wicked for me. If the goddams and the Burgundians do not make an end of me, the French will. But for my voices I should lose all heart. That is why I had to come here alone after all that great splendour of the coronation. Listen. It is in the bells I hear my voices; but today, when all the bells rang, I could hear nothing but jangling. But here, where the bells came suddenly in the silence, and the echoes linger, or in the fields, where they come from a distance through the quiet of the countryside, my voices are in them. [*The cathedral clock chimes the quarter*] Hark. [*She becomes rapt*]. Did you hear it say "Dear-child-of-God"—just what you said? At the half hour it will say "Jean-nette-be-bold." At the three quarters they will say "All-shall-go-well." But it is at the hour, when the	Jack: the world is too wicked for me. If the goddams and the Burgundians do not make an end of me, the French will. Only for my voices I should lose all heart. That is why I had to steal away to pray here alone after the coronation. I'll tell you something, Jack. It is in the bells I hear my voices. Not to-day when they all rang: that was nothing but jangling. But here in this corner where the bells come down from heaven, and the echoes linger, or in the fields, where they come from a distance through the quiet of the countryside, my voices are in them. [*The cathedral clock chimes the quarter*] Hark! [*She becomes rapt*] Do you hear? "Dear-child-of-God": just what you said. At the half-hour they will say "Be-brave-go-on." At the three quarters they will say "I-am-thy-Help." But it is at the hour, when the great bell goes after "God-will-save-

great bell goes after "God-will-save-France" that St Margaret and St Catherine and sometimes even the blessed Michael will say things that I cannot tell beforehand.

France": it is then that St Margaret and St Catherine and sometimes even the blessed Michael will say things that I cannot tell beforehand.

The alterations, though slight, are clearly rhetorical. The immediate source for the idea expressed was probably Murray, where the testament of Jean Waterin, a labourer of Greux, states, "Often when she was in the fields and heard the bells ring she would drop on her knees."[21] While that of Simonin Musnier, a labourer of Domremy, adds, "When the church bells rang I have seen her kneel down and make the sign of the cross."[22]

But Shaw may have privately admired the idea as it was elaborated upon by Percy Mackaye in *Jeanne d'Arc*, where Jeanne, quizzed about the angels she has seen, replies:

> But oftenest I hear them speak; I call them "My Voices," and I hear them when the bells Are ringing—more at Matins and at Vespers Than other hours.[23]

Of course, Mackaye is obviously using Murray closely too, which is why he echoes Joan's statement that the "voices" called her "Daughter of God" by making the two voices call "Daughter of God, go forth!" (which is similar to Shaw's interpretation).[24]

Joan's second long speech of the scene also concerns the bells, and Shaw makes her as specific as Mackaye's heroine:

> Joan = They do come to you; but you do not hear them. You have not sat in the field in the evening listening for them. When the angelus rings you cross yourself and have done with it; but if you prayed from your hearts and listened to the thrilling of the bells in the air after they stop ringing you would hear the voices as well as I do. (fol. 37)

Although Shaw had adapted his idea from the comments of Waterin and Musnier, he perhaps did not have his copy of Murray with him in Ireland; and he seems to have discussed Joan and her bells with Father Leonard there during his revision of these scenes, and also sought the priest's advice during his writing of the Epilogue, prompting the following comment in a letter from Father Leonard, dated 17 September 1923, the day before Shaw returned to England: "I looked up the 'angelus' point. You have all the historical evidence you want for letting her hear the bells ring."[25] We are speaking, however, not of history, but of poetry.

Eighteen months before Shaw began his play he received a pathetic, wild, begging letter, from a young Bulgarian woman, Franzi Trajanowa, most poetically phrased, begging for money to restore the sight of her blind writer-husband. One wonders whether the echo of some of her phrases was in Shaw's mind when he wrote Joan's dialogue in Scene V. Particularly worth comparison are Joan's speeches about the bells and this from Franzi Trajanowa's letter: "And I lifted up my work-worn hands to God, and begged the Almighty in my despair to save my husband's soul. Then my suffering ears heard the voice of an angel that sounded like silver bells. The bells spoke the celebrated name of 'Bernard Shaw,' and my eyes fell on your picture." She again catches Joan's cadence when she speaks of the Bulgarian wars: "To everybody's dismay these wars ended sadly and after ten years of bloody struggle we have only succeeded in losing more of our brothers. That hurts very much, and it hurts too that the big powers abuse our weakness, want to disarm us, so that the greedy enemy, like a herd of hungry wolves may fall on us and swallow us entirely."[26]

It is impossible to read Scene V without becoming aware of its poetry and its operatic quality. Indeed, John Rosselli, in criticizing the John Fernald production of *Saint Joan*,[27] reminds us that Shaw's style owes much to Mozartian opera, and illustrates the indebtedness by setting out the first of Dunois' two long speeches in Scene V, beginning "I think that God was on your side," not as poetry (which, he says, it is not), but as prose admirably designed for speaking in the theatre. The source for this speech is Dunois himself, who began his deposition at Orleans in 1455, with the words, "I think that Jeanne was sent by God, and that her behaviour in war was a fact divine rather than human." Shaw, in transposing this to dialogue in his play, is able to combine the soldierly bluffness of Dunois with a poetic rhythm which maintains the tension in this most poetic scene:

> I think that God was on your side—for I have not forgotten how the wind changed and how our hearts changed when you came; and by my faith I shall never deny that it was in your sign that we conquered. (fols. 37–38)

As Rosselli points out, at the conclusion of Dunois' speech ("and serve us right!"), Joan interrupts with the word "But"—only to have Dunois retort "Sh! I have not finished," making, on sound operatic principles, a bridge to the second half of his speech, which concerns the part he played in Joan's victories. The alterations in these speeches by Dunois are slight, and made to improve the rhythm of the lines. The line, "But I tell you as a soldier that God does not fight men's battles for them," becomes, "But I tell you as a soldier that God is no man's daily drudge, and no maid's either." While the line, "For the people will run after the Maid and her miracles and not after the Bastard's strategy or his ordering of his troops and finding food for them," becomes "For the people will run after the Maid and her miracles and not after the Bastard's hard work finding troops for her and feeding them," the rhythm of which is helped by the alliteration. Rosselli points out accurately that Shaw's speeches do not need to be long to be operatic:

> The rest of the Cathedral Scene, after Dunois' speech, is almost wholly so. There is a short aria for Joan and another for Dunois, with a bridge of dialogue in between; then a sort of quartet when Charles, Dunois, and the Archbishop in turn refuse to help Joan, followed by the Archbishop's long denunciation, which Dunois and Charles break into briefly. All this leads up to Joan's long aria and her exit.[28]

The aria in question, truly the most moving and beautiful one in the play, underwent extensive revision before it assumed its final form. Again for comparison let us place side by side the transcript of the original shorthand and what it became in the printed version:

British Library Add. MSS 45923, fols. 40–41

Dunois = That is the truth Joan. Heed it.

Joan = Oh how well I know it is true! There is no help, no counsel, in any of you. I am alone: I have always been alone. My father threatened to drown me, and told my brothers and sisters to drown me if I was disobedient and did not stay to mind his sheep whilst France was bleeding to death. I left the farm because France had no friends there: our people might perish provided the lambs were safe. I thought France would have friends at the court of the king of France; and I found only wolves fighting for pieces of her poor torn body. I thought God would have friends everywhere, because he is the friend of everyone; and I thought in my innocence that you who now cast me out would be like a strong tower to

Saint Joan
(London: Constable & Co., 1924)

DUNOIS. That is the truth, Joan. Heed it.

JOAN. Where would you all have been now if I had heeded that sort of truth? There is no help, no counsel, in any of you. Yes: I am alone on earth: I have always been alone. My father told my brothers to drown me if I would not stay to mind his sheep while France was bleeding to death: France might perish if only our lambs were safe. I thought France would have friends at the court of the king of France; and I find only wolves fighting for pieces of her poor torn body. I thought God would have friends everywhere, because He is the friend of everyone; and in my innocence I believed that you who now cast me out would be like strong towers to keep harm from me. But I am wiser now; and nobody is any keep harm from me. You think you can terrify me by telling me me (sic) that I am alone. Yes: I am alone; but France is alone, and God is alone; and what is my solitude before the solitude of my country and my God? I see now that the loneliness of God is his strength: what would he be if he listened to your petty counsels? Well, my loneliness shall be my strength too: it is better to be alone with God: his friendship will not fail me, nor his counsel, nor his love. In his strength I will dare, and dare, and dare, until I die. I will go out now to the common people and let the love in their eyes comfort me for the hate in yours. You will all be glad to see me burnt; but if I go through the fire I shall go through it to their hearts for ever and ever. And so, God be with me.

the worse for being wiser. Do not think you can frighten me by telling me that I am alone. France is alone; and God is alone; and what is my loneliness before the loneliness of my country and my God? I see now that the loneliness of God is His strength: what would He be if He listened to your jealous little counsels? Well, my loneliness shall be my strength too: it is better to be alone with God: His friendship will not fail me, nor His counsel, nor His love. In His strength I will dare, and dare, and dare, until I die. I will go out now to the common people, and let the love in their eyes comfort me for the hate in yours. You will all be glad to see me burnt; but if I go through the fire I shall go through it to their hearts for ever and ever. And so, God be with me!

The rather startling information about Joan's father Shaw took from Murray, where Jeanne reports:

> I have heard my mother say that my father told my brothers: "Truly if I thought this thing would happen that I have dreamed about my daughter, I would wish you to drown her; and, if you would not do it, I would drown her myself!"[29]

Jeanne, however, partially absolves her father in her next sentence, stating simply:

> He nearly lost his senses when I went to Vaucouleurs.

The appropriate simile of France as a sheep beset by hungry wolves may have been suggested by Trajanowa's letter quoted above, but most accounts of Joan of Arc tend to use the shepherd metaphor, no doubt because of its religious connotation. Quicherat in his *Aperçus*, speaking of Jeanne's birth, reports that "les loups s'adoucissaient devant les moutons de son troupeau."[30] Southey likens France to a sheep:

> Unhappy France!
> Fiercer than evening wolves thy bitter foes
> Rush o'er the land, and desolate and kill.[31]

And Mark Twain, prompted by the recollection that during the bitterest winter that had visited France in five hundred years, "The dead lay in heaps about the streets, and *wolves entered the city in daylight and devoured them,*" continues the metaphor by stating, "Ah, France had fallen low, so low! For more than three quarters of a century the English fangs had been buried in her flesh."[32]

The final concept in Joan's speech, namely that "the loneliness of God is His strength," is the development of an idea expressed by Ibsen at the end of *An Enemy of the People*, written in 1882. Interestingly enough, Ibsen also begins by using the "wolf" metaphor, this time for the misguided yet savage conformists who have rejected his hero, Stockmann, and who are seeking to drive him from the town. Stockmann declares his intention of defying the people, of setting up a school where he will teach children to be "free high-minded men."

MORTEN: But what are we to do when we've grown into free and high-minded men?

DR. STOCKMANN: Drive all the wolves out to the far west, boys!

(EILEF looks rather doubtful; MORTEN jumps about shouting "Hurrah!")

MRS. STOCKMANN: If only the wolves don't drive you out, Thomas.

DR. STOCKMANN: Are you quite mad, Katrina! Drive me out! Now that I am the strongest man in the town?

MRS. STOCKMANN: The strongest — now?

DR. STOCKMANN: Yes, I venture to say this: that now I am one of the strongest men in the whole world.

MORTEN: I say, what fun!

DR. STOCKMANN (in a subdued voice): Hush; you mustn't speak about it yet: but I have made a great discovery.

MRS. STOCKMANN: What, another?

DR. STOCKMANN: Yes, of course! (Gathers them about him, and speaks confidentially): This is what I have discovered, you see: the strongest man in the world is he who stands most alone.[33]

The chief difference between Joan and Stockmann is their reaction to "the common people." In Joan's time the common people could only look on, wonder at, and perhaps sympathize with, her plight, not having the power to prevent it.

By the nineteenth century, however, the common people, although having more of a voice in public affairs, have become regular readers of Hovstad's newspaper, and are simply swayed by the political psychology of Peter the bureaucrat to accept the verdict of their "superiors" and condemn the doctor. Consequently Shaw, although a socialist, had always endorsed Ibsen's view: "Whatever clatter we may make for a time with our filing through feudal serf collars and kicking off old mercantilist fetters, we shall never march a step forward except at the heels of 'the strongest man, he who is able to stand alone,' and to turn his back on 'the damned compact Liberal majority.'"[34] A reinforcement of this idea, causing it to surface in *Saint Joan*, may well have been the identification each author felt with his principal protagonist at the time the two plays were written: Ibsen had written his following the public's rejection of *Ghosts*; Shaw had written *Saint Joan* after twenty-one years of fruitless dramatic persuasion.[35]

4

A Saint to the Stake

The Trial Scene of *Saint Joan*, Scene VI,[1] is perhaps the greatest scene in the play, and yet Hesketh Pearson reports that Shaw himself told Sybil Thorndike, "The trial scene is merely a report of the actual trial. I have used Joan's very words."[2] Nevertheless, as John Mason Brown cautions, "Count this among the least reliable of Shavian utterances. In *Saint Joan* Shaw matters at every turn and with the turn of almost every phrase."[3] Since Shaw was committed to establishing that Joan received a fair trial, in the teeth of the tradition that she was unfairly judged, it is perhaps hardly surprising that critics have taken issue with his statement that he merely transcribed the facts of the trial. Arnold Lunn, writing as early as 1926, states:

> At the risk of being damned as an uncultured critic with no historical imagination, I must still deny that the Inquisition was just or humane, and must confess to a sneaking suspicion that Mr. Shaw, both in his play and in his preface, has been less anxious to interpret the past in accordance with the available evidence than to find yet another excuse for battering at his favourite Aunt Sallies, "bothered Majors" presiding over court martials, martial law, vaccinationists, the Black and Tans, and Englishmen in general.[4]

Others have agreed. Treading a thin line, and giving Shaw his due, Christopher Hollis nevertheless differs with him on theological grounds. He accepts Shaw's view on papal infallibility, and thus, one might imagine, vindicates the right of the individual to private revelation from God, but then spoils his magnanimity by saying: "If, as a result of revelation which pretends to be divine, a person ascribes to God a purpose different in any way from that which the Church teaches Him to possess, then the Church has the right to condemn that pretended revelation."[5] This is a remarkable statement, which suggests that Hollis is a spiritual descendant of Cauchon himself!

The rancorous grumblings of J. M. Robertson in his 1925 book *Mr. Shaw and "The Maid"* are similarly self-defeating. He carps at small alterations of fact in

the Trial Scene; and that his attack on Shaw should have been so warmly supported by no less a critic than T. S. Eliot in his review of Robertson's book,[6] must
be attributed to a rare confusion of ethics and aesthetics in Eliot. In any case, the
nodding of so Homeric a critic (who once dismissed *Hamlet* as "most certainly an
artistic failure") was atoned for later in *Poetry and Drama* when he went so far as
to admit that *Murder in the Cathedral* may have been written "slightly under the
influence of *Saint Joan*"; and presumably he had forgotten it entirely when in
1951 he classified Congreve and Shaw as the "two greatest prose stylists in the
drama."

As far as the alterations of fact are concerned, the only substantive criticism
made by Robertson, Shaw was perfectly well aware of the artistic licence he had
taken: "Joan's unconscious confessions of heresy at her trial, her recantation, her
relapse and her execution, occupied several days. On the stage they occupy forty
minutes; but nothing essential is misrepresented; and nothing is omitted except
the adjournments and matters irrelevant to the final issue."[7] Hollis was to claim,
correctly, that Shaw had omitted Cauchon's refusal to allow Joan's appeals to the
Pope and the Council of Basle, and the attempt to suppress record of those
appeals. But Shaw's primary source doesn't make much of this; and Shaw makes
Joan hint at it when he has her complain about being in the hands of the English
when she should be in the hands of the Church. Few of the play's other critics
complain of this omission, although fewer can be found as positive as J. H. Buckland, who believes that Shaw has "placed the historian under an obligation to the
drama and the stage."[8]

In fact, the trials of Jeanne d'Arc lasted from 21 February to 30 May 1431, and
Shaw chooses his dialogue from questions and testimony scattered over the three-
month period.

Even allowing for its dramatic impact, such necessary compression of fact does
result in losses. Chief of these is the cumulative effect of the repeated hearings
and incessant questioning. Secondly, one misses the carefully chosen settings in
which the real trials were held—chosen perhaps from a desire on the part of
Jeanne's judges to awe her into submission. She was first arraigned, for example,
in the Chapel Royal of Rouen Castle: a dignified and symbolic setting. Later she
was interviewed in prison; and on Wednesday, 9 May, she was interrogated in the
great tower of the castle, where the instruments of torture were kept, and here
she was threatened with torture in the presence of the executioners. Shaw seems
to have been aware of the sacrifices he had to make in the name of artistic unity,
for he includes as many elements as he can, either in fact or by reference, drawn
from both the trial ex officio and the trial in ordinary.

The diffuse nature of the references may be one reason why Shaw (unusually,
for him) seems to have begun without a detailed picture of his stage in mind, in
spite of a print of the "Court of Justice" (from a miniature by Jean Fouquet) in

Murray. For although in the printed version of his play Shaw sets the trial firmly enough,

Rouen, 30 May, 1431

which was the day of Joan's death (there was, in fact, no trial on that day, only the reading of the sentence), originally he had begun much more vaguely:

> *A room in the castle, arranged for a trial at law. There are two presidents' seats side by side, raised above the others. There is a table for the scribes. Warwick comes in with his page.* (fol. 42)

Notwithstanding the vague start, however, there are few significant alterations to the dialogue of Scene VI. Of interest to the above critics, who complain of Shaw's unfair "impartiality," in his treatment of the trial, might be the following deletion of dialogue. In the first draft, after Warwick's expression of relief at the news that the trial is about to proceed after so long a delay, he feels moved to apologize for the conduct of some of the British soldiers:

> Warwick = I will not attempt to conceal from you that our patience was becoming strained. In fact I have to apologize to you, Monseigneur, for the conduct of some of our soldiers, encouraged, I regret to say, by the Earl of Stafford. One of your distinguished lawyers, Master Lohier, had to come to me for protection. Also a priest. I saw to it that they were no further molested. The priest's name was Loyseleur, I think. I cannot excuse the threats of drowning addressed to Master Lohier; but Loyseleur seems to have been disguised in some compromising way.
>
> Cauchon = Loyseleur was disguised to gain the Maid's confidence: a stratagem which has no peril for an innocent woman. I will ask your lordship to take special order for his protection. But as to Lohier, we are very well rid of him. He is a conceited anticlerical lawyer who declares that all the proceedings against the Maid are illegal and should be begun all over again.
>
> Warwick = I will see that he troubles you no more, my lord.
>
> Cauchon = No no; I have asked him to be present at the trial; and if he chooses to leave the town instead that is his affair not mine. But he must not be coerced in any way. I think his points are worthless; but I am determined that the woman shall have a fair hearing. The mercy of the Church is not a mockery my lord. (fol. 43)

The specious way in which Cauchon in this extract differentiates between Lohier and Loyseleur,[9] excusing the latter and calling for his protection, while utterly condemning the "anti-clerical" lawyer, makes deeply ironic his final remark. It is instructive to see what this passage became in its reduced form:

> WARWICK. I will not attempt to conceal from you that our patience was becoming strained.
> CAUCHON. So I gathered from the threats of your soldiers to drown those of our people who favor The Maid.[10]
> WARWICK. Dear me! At all events their intentions were friendly to you, my lord.
> CAUCHON [sternly] I hope not. I am determined that the woman shall have a fair hearing. The justice of the Church is not a mockery, my lord.[11]

In this brief exchange, Cauchon is clearly the winner; and it is worth mentioning in this regard that the conflict necessary to drama almost insists upon a sparring match. In the original extract the conflict is slight, arising from the opposing views of Lohier and Loyseleur held by Warwick and Cauchon, who are nevertheless still in agreement on the main issue. The replacement roots the conflict deeper: in national distrust for one another, and the embarrassment and irritation of a sincere churchman who is apparently allowing himself to be used by a faithless politician because, though he may privately deplore the means, he favours the end. The alteration, then, strengthens the dramatic structure, as well as the character of Cauchon.

Shortly after this, in the original manuscript, d'Estivet is made to amplify Cauchon's point about Lohier:

> This man Lohier has dared to say that we are acting from hate and therefore, like Pilate, (whose damnation may he share for his falsehood) he will wash his hands and leave the town; but as God is my witness he lies. (fol. 43)

But after the earlier excision, the speech becomes superfluous, though its "key" is correct. Accordingly, Shaw generalized it to,

> Men have dared to say that we are acting from hate; but God is our witness that they lie.

It is also of interest to note that Shaw's first intention was to bring in Joan, the accused, much earlier in the scene, before, in fact, the Inquisitor's long speech. Her entrance was planned to follow the duologue between Cauchon and Warwick, part of which is mentioned above, and which originally concluded as follows:

Warwick = Well, by all means do your best for her if you are quite sure that it will be of no avail. I should be sorry to have to act without the blessing of the Church.

Cauchon = And yet they say that Englishmen are hypocrites! You play for your side, my lord, even at the peril of your soul. I cannot but admire such devotion; but I dare not go so far myself. I fear damnation—perhaps, because *I* believe in it. Come, let us take our places and begin the trial. [He moves to his presidential chair].

Warwick = One must not be selfish in politics: it is a luxury denied to the governing class, my lord. I will send in your people to you [he goes out].

Cauchon [seated] I thank your lordship. [To the Inquisitor, who is taking the seat on his right] What scoundrels the English governing classes are!

The Inquisitor = Yes: they do not seem to understand.

The court assembles. The scribes, including Chaplain de Stogumber, take their places at the table and produce their parchments and writing materials. D'Estivet also places himself at the table.

Cauchon [*to one of the entering Canons*] Master de Courcelles: you are a Canon of Paris. Have you any news from the university?

Courcelles = I have, my lord. [*He goes to the presidential chair and whispers to the bishop. The Inquisitor joins in this whispered conversation*].
Joan is brought in, in her soldier's dress, with some remnants of finery still left, but much the worse for wear. She is herself worn by imprisonment, but not cast down. She takes her place with as much assurance as the bishop. (fol. 44)

Now although Shaw did not entirely delete this section, nevertheless, even before the revision in Ireland, he had obviously determined to delay the arrival of his main protagonist until he had more fully created the character of the Inquisitor, if not of the Inquisition. And this he does by first showing that gentleman in conflict—albeit genial conflict—with two rather pedantic clerics in the court: de Courcelles and de Stogumber. For this purpose, Shaw makes use of yet another fact he found in Murray: the reduction in the number of articles prepared by the Promoter which form the act of accusation against Joan. Originally seventy in number, these were reduced to twelve.[12] By using this information, Shaw also brings about a comic reduction in stature of the French Canon and the English Chaplain; though the jokes at their expense, however Shavian they sound, are selected from the actual articles: the belief that St. Margaret should have spoken in English (appearing on page 40 of Murray), and the comically inappropriate concern over the horse belonging to the Bishop of Senlis (on page 51). Apart from promoting laughter at the expense of the two clerics, Shaw is effecting an important contrast here: the Inquisitor is neither pedant nor humourless fanatic; on the contrary he is mild-mannered, witty, and above all reasonable. His gentle rebuke of the two indignant prelates establishes his authority, and paves the way for his splendid flight of oratory which covers two and a half pages in the printed text.

In content this speech is pure Shaw: nothing like this interpretation of history is to be found in the sources, although the tone, grave yet gentle, and one or two of the admonitions are not unlike those in the public admonition by Cauchon on 2 May 1431 in the Castle of Rouen:

> ...and before We come to a final decision, many honest men, conscientious and wise, have thought it would be well to seek by all means to instruct her on the points in which she seems to be lacking, and to reinstate her in the way and knowledge of the truth. This result We have always desired, and We ardently desire it still. For We ought all to bend ourselves thereto, We who live in the Church, and in the ministration of holy things; We ought to strive to show to this woman with all gentleness that she is, by her words and by her actions, outside the Faith, the truth, and religion, and to warn her charitably to think of her salvation.[13]

Shaw's Inquisitor, too, correctly identified as Brother John Lemaître of the Order of St. Dominic, is somewhat similar to the man who cautiously acceded to the order in the letters patent from the Chief Inquisitor, and reluctantly attended the trial, delaying his appearance as long as he could, the fair-minded man who interceded on behalf of those clerics who were threatened by Cauchon for advising the Maid to submit to the Pope.[14]

The Inquisitor's speech, in spite of its amazing reasonableness, is not, as some critics have averred, a defence of the Inquisition; nor yet it seems to me is it entirely a subtle attack upon that institution, though there is sophistry in the Inquisitor's argument for those to find who will. As William Searle points out: "the soundness of his reasoning cannot rescue him from the falsity of his position, which requires him to distinguish between [false and true prophets] without being divinely inspired himself."[15] It is, therefore, a demonstration of the fact that unblessed with the benefit of hindsight, any one of his audience, faced with the trial of Joan, would have found the issues far less black and white than they appear five hundred years later.[16]

Indeed, Cauchon's lines immediately following the Inquisitor's speech seem to sum it up: "I do not see how any sane man could disagree with a word that has fallen from you." The persuasiveness of the Inquisitor is reminiscent of that of the Knights as they come forward to address the audience at the end of *Murder in The Cathedral*. No doubt Eliot was reminded of the speech in *Saint Joan* as he wrote this part of his own play. For the Knights at this point, like the Inquisitor, have the ability to liberate their play from its temporal setting, and thus to involve, and even indict, the audience with the murder of its principal figure; an even more powerful device in Shaw than Eliot, because the partial acquiescence we give by acknowledging the reasonableness of the Inquisitor's speech is to a murder as yet uncommitted, and therefore theoretically still preventable.

Cauchon's speech, however, which forms a bridge between the Inquisitor's closing remarks and the arrival of Joan herself, puts the audience firmly back on her side, both by its savage emotionalism, and by the nature of the "new heresy" of Protestantism, against which Cauchon inveighs so loudly. From the (this time correct) arrival of Joan, Shaw's earlier claim to have reported the trial accurately comes back into focus; for there is no doubt that the trial proper is based in every particular upon the *Procès* as it is reported by Quicherat and translated by Murray. Practically every line that Joan utters can be found there, as can many of the lines of her persecutors.

When she enters, which she does with approximately the same stage directions as originally devised for her, the Inquisitor remarks upon how pale she looks, an additional kindly injunction to "sit down" being added to the revised version. He asks her if she is well. Her reply, "I am well enough," is close to Jeanne's reply of 27 February 1431, "I am as well as can be," in answer to Maître Beaupère's similar opening question. Shaw's heroine goes on to declare, however, that the Bishop had sent her some carp, and that it had made her ill. This is what Jeanne alleges on page 253 of Murray: "She replied that some carp had been sent her by the Bishop of Beauvais, and that she doubted this was the cause of her illness." Unlike Mark Twain, however, who also uses this incident, and says that she "charged Cauchon with trying to kill her with a poisoned fish,"[17] Shaw more accurately writes in accordance with the evidence of the doctor, Maître Guillaume Delachambre, who reports:

> The Earl of Warwick told us that Jeanne had been ill and that we had been sent for to give her all our attention, for the King would not, for anything, that she should die a natural death: he had bought her too dear for that, and he intended that she should die at the hands of justice, and should be burnt.[18]

This is in line with Joan's next speech, where she says the English sent a doctor to cure her, but that he "only called me filthy names." A sentence added to the revised version is:

> But he was forbidden to bleed me because the silly people believe that a witch's witchery leaves her if she is bled.

This is not what the real doctor reported: he alleged that his prescription that she should be bled was set aside by Warwick, who said "Away with your bleeding! . . .

She is artful, and might kill herself." The doctor also alleges that it was Maître Guillaume D'Estivet who used evil words against Jeanne, "calling her . . . and a paillard," presumably the "filthy names" to which Shaw's Joan alludes. Her question "Why do you leave me in the hands of the English?" comes from page 74 of Murray (Joan's testimony on Wednesday, 14 March 1431) where she says, "I had rather die than be in the hands of my enemies, the English." The line "Why must I be chained by the feet to a log of wood?" in Shaw's play, is paralleled by "And as she complained that she had been fastened with chains and fetters of iron" (Murray, page 7); while the subsequent question in *Saint Joan*, "Are you afraid I will fly away?" is a simple transcription of "I shall not fly away!" on page 49 of Murray. De Courcelles rebukes her by saying, "When you were left unchained, did you not try to escape by jumping from a tower sixty feet high?"[19] Attempting to escape, Joan actually did leap from the tower of Beaurevoir and injured herself, explaining (on page 54 of Murray):

> When I knew that the English were come to take me I was very angry; nevertheless, my Voices forbade me many times to leap. In the end, for fear of the English, I leapt, and commended myself to God and Our Lady. I was wounded.

The question "Why did you jump from the tower?" which is asked repeatedly by Shaw's D'Estivet was asked just as insistently on 14 March 1431; and to D'Estivet's sharp rephrasing of the question, "You tried to escape?" Joan's reply "Of course I did," captures the pertness of Jeanne's response on page 7 of Murray, "It is true I wished to escape; and so I wish still: is not this lawful for all prisoners?" This last Shaw transmutes figuratively into "If you leave the door of a cage open the bird will fly out," which is both a reprise of the image in the Loire Scene, and an anticipation of Joan's reason for tearing up her recantation.

After this brief exchange of questions, it is pointed out by the Inquisitor that the trial is not yet in order, the proceedings not having been formally opened:

> The time for questions is after she has sworn on the Gospels to tell us the whole truth.

This reference to "the whole truth" prompts from Joan a response that Jeanne repeatedly gave during the trial:

> I will not tell you all; I have not leave; my oath does not touch on that.[20]

Shaw, who only presents one of the many hearings, makes her say:

You say this to me every time. I have said again and again that I will tell you all that concerns this trial. But I cannot tell you the whole truth: God does not allow the whole truth to be told. (fol. 49)

And Joan's exasperation, which builds during this section ("I have sworn as much as I will swear; and I will swear no more," which derives from "I swore yesterday: that should be enough"—Murray, page 9) culminates in "If you were to tear me limb from limb and separate my soul from my body you would get nothing out of me beyond what I have told you." And this is almost a direct quote from Murray (page 117):

Truly if you were to tear me limb from limb, and separate soul from body, I will tell you nothing more.

Even the sentiment expressed by Joan at the end of that speech, that she cannot bear to be hurt, and will confess to anything under torture, but that she will take it all back again afterwards, is a rather more humorous version of Jeanne's "and, if I were to say anything else, I should afterwards declare that you made me say it by force."

The quarrel over the use of torture, which Shaw interjects at this point, is clearly meant to capture, however briefly, the events of 9 and 12 May, on the first of which dates Jeanne was threatened with torture, and on the second of which her judges met with the assessors to discuss whether or not she should be tortured. Fourteen assessors were consulted, only two of whom, Aubert Morel and Thomas de Courcelles, were in favour of it. Loyseleur considered it "a salutary medicine for her soul," but nevertheless agreed that it should not be adopted. Shaw accurately makes Courcelles the spokesman for the rack; and also has him outvoted. This is a further opportunity to develop the kindly character of the Inquisitor, who yet again pours oil on troubled waters, counselling de Courcelles not to be moved by "the rough side of a shepherd lass's tongue." This, in turn, gives Shaw both the opportunity of stressing anew the fact that Joan's social status was higher than the description "shepherd lass" would suggest,[21] and a chance to demonstrate once more her fatal boldness in the face of her persecutors. Though she admits she has helped with the sheep, she adds, "I will do a lady's work in the house — spin or weave—against any woman in Lorraine." Shaw later corrected that to "against any woman in Rouen," and did so, it seems, with Murray open in front of him, at page 9; where Jeanne says:

Yes, I learnt to spin and to sew; in sewing and spinning I fear no woman in Rouen.

At this point in Shaw's play, Cauchon interrupts, to complain rightly that they are wasting time on trifles. There follows some heavy questioning of the accused, questioning which did indeed take place on 17 March 1431 and on the last day of March (Easter evening). On the last-named date the following question was asked of Jeanne:

> Will you refer yourself to the judgement of the Church on earth for all you have said or done, be it good or bad? Especially will you refer to the Church the cases, crimes, and offences which are imputed to you and everything which touches on this Trial?

Cauchon's question is imitative even to the very rhythms of the original:

> Will you for all you have said and done, be it good or bad, accept the judgment of God's Church on earth? More especially as to the acts and words that are imputed to you in this trial by the Promoter here, will you submit your case to the inspired interpretation of the Church Militant?

Joan's reply in Shaw's play also comes from the same page in Murray:[22]

> Joan = I am a faithful child of the Church. I will obey the Church—
> Cauchon [hopefully leaning forward] You will?
> Joan = —provided it does not command anything impossible. (fol. 50)

This was a cardinal point; and Shaw indicates this by following Joan's remark with the stage directions: *Cauchon sits back in his chair with a heavy sigh. The Inquisitor purses his lips and frowns. Ladvenu shakes his head pitifully.* And although we have no record of the reaction of her judges, the same incriminating statement was made by Jeanne, who said:

> On all that I am asked I will refer to the Church Militant, provided they do not command anything impossible.

In short, the brilliance of Shaw in this scene lies not in the creation but the selection of dialogue from his principal source. He clearly read Murray with his critical faculties astretch, alert for fine lines and central issues; for the best and apparently most Shavian lines in the Trial Scene are all to be found in Murray's translation of Quicherat. The exactness of Shaw's transcript also speaks to his admiration for Joan herself, while additional proof of his approval of the material he borrows is to be found in the onstage reactions (like the one noted above) which Shaw adds. Another example of this is in his use of Joan's most famous reply to her enraged accuser Cauchon,[23] who asks: "Dare you pretend, after what you have said, that you are in a state of grace?"

> Joan = If I am not, may God bring me to it: if I am, may God keep me in it! (fol. 51)

This beautiful reply, most powerful in the theatre, is taken from page 18 of Murray:

> "Do you know if you are in the grace of God?"
> "If I am not, may God place me there; if I am, may God so keep me."

That Shaw himself was pleased with Joan at this point is evident from the fact that he makes Ladvenu comment: "That is a very good reply, my lord," though even here he has warrant in Murray, when, on another occasion, after Jeanne had declared that in all things she waited on Our Lord, a response is noted in the court record: "That is an answer of great weight."

Shaw points up the beauty of Joan's reply about the grace of God by a telling moment of anti-climax. Courcelles asks, "Were you in a state of grace when you stole the Bishop's horse?" The collapse into absurdity is Shaw's reproduction of another thread that he found running through Murray, one as insistent as the brilliance of the Maid in the face of the sophistries of her accusers; and that is the vein of genuine stupidity that regularly reveals itself in the triviality of their questioning. The intellectual disparity between Joan and her judges has often been noted: indeed it is this that renders absurd such judgements of Shaw's play as that given by R. Ellis Roberts in the *Bookman*'s review of its English performance, where he claims that Shaw's Saint Joan "read 'Sesame and Lilies,' and Tennyson's 'Idylls' and loved the 'Angel in the House.' She was charming and she may have been Catholic, but she was neither peasant nor mediaevalist."[24] Such a view of Shaw's character, apart from being an affront to common sense, fails to realize that the real Jeanne d'Arc in many ways *was* foreign to her century; that it was so evident to those of her contemporaries who tried her that she *was* neither peasant nor medievalist that they acquiesced in her burning. In order to stress the vast differences between the attitude of Joan and her judges, Shaw at this point juxtaposes her best responses with their most feeble accusations.

Cauchon, who is exempted from ridicule in this instance, impatiently breaks in to the furor over the Bishop's horse, and again the Inquisitor calms the passions of the court, before directing the Promoter to take the questioning. The latter, sharing Cauchon's impatience on the minor charges, wishes to concentrate instead upon "two very horrible and blasphemous crimes which she does not deny." After such powerful epithets, it is with some surprise that the audience learns that these crimes are first that she talks to spirits, which makes her a sorceress; and second that she habitually wears male clothing. But in fact these *were* the two charges which the court could not forgive. In some way the two charges seem to have been connected in the minds of Jeanne's judges; and Shaw senses this. Certainly her accusers (Shaw gives the honour to Courcelles) seem to want to trick the young girl before them into an immoral utterance by asking her:

> Courcelles = How do you know that the spirit which appears to you is the archangel is an archangel (sic)? Does he not appear to you as a naked man?
> Joan = Do you think God cannot afford to clothe him? (fol. 52)

This exchange, which sets the assessors and the audience smiling sympathetically at the Maid's discretion, again is a verbatim transcript of what took place in Rouen in 1431:

> "In what likeness did St. Michael appear to you?"
> "I did not see a crown, I know nothing of his dress."
> "Was he naked?"
> "Do you think God has not wherewithal to clothe him?"

So far as *her* clothing is concerned, to her accusers, who were at a loss to know why she should assume male dress "by order of God," Shaw makes Joan more explicit than she was at the trial:

> Ladvenu = Can you suggest to us one good reason why an angel of God should give you such shameless advice?
> Joan = Why, yes; what can be plainer commonsense? I am a soldier living among soldiers. If I dress as a woman they will think of me as a woman; and how then could I live among them? If I dress as a soldier they think of me as a soldier, and I can live with them as with my brothers. That is why St Catherine tells me I must not dress as a woman until she gives me leave.
> Courcelles = When will she give you leave?
> Joan = When you take me out of the hands of the English soldiers.[25] (fol. 52)

Jeanne, more simply, excused herself for having resumed male attire by saying:

> ...it is more lawful and suitable for me to resume it and to wear man's dress, being with men, than to have a woman's dress.[26]

Indeed, Brother Ysambard de la Pierre testified that she had been assaulted in the prison during the brief period when she had dressed as a woman:

I and many others were present when Jeanne excused herself for having dressed again as a man, saying and affirming publicly that the English had done to her great wrong and violence, when she was wearing a woman's dress.

The climax of Shaw's Trial Scene is Joan's collapse into despair and disbelief in her voices, and her recantation; followed almost at once by her tearing up of that recantation so recently signed; which action leads to her sentencing and immediate execution. This is where Shaw takes the greatest liberties with the sequence of historical events.

The facts are these. On 24 May, the trial of Jeanne d'Arc was concluded, and the sentence was being read aloud to her when she interrupted and suddenly announced that she would hold all that the Church ordained, and that inasmuch as the clergy decided her apparitions and revelations were not to be believed, she would not believe them. She then made her recantation, was declared free from the danger of excommunication, but sentenced to life imprisonment. Later the same day she was visited in prison by Jean Lemaître and a group of her judges and warned that she must not return to her errors on pain of being abandoned altogether by the Church. On this occasion she was told to resume women's garments, and when these were brought she did so, also submitting to having her hair cut.

Four days later the same group of judges returned to the prison to see "the state and disposition of her soul." Jeanne had relapsed and was again dressed like a man. In response to their rebukes, she accused her judges of having broken promises made to her, that she should not be kept in irons, and that she should be allowed to attend Mass. She was, apparently, very spirited on this occasion, saying, "I would rather die than be in irons! but if I am allowed to go to Mass, and am taken out of irons and put into a gracious prison . . . I will be good and do as the Church wills." She also stated that all she had said previously had been for fear of the fire. And she cried out, "I have damned myself to save my life!"

The following day, a meeting was held in the Archiepiscopal Manor of Rouen, attended by her judges and forty assessors. First, all the happenings from 19 May onward were reviewed; then each assessor was asked for his recommendation. The consensus was that Jeanne should be abandoned to the secular authority. Accordingly, she was summoned to appear in the old market place on Wednesday, 30 May 1431, the order being signed at 7:00 a.m. that very morning. She was taken to the market place and placed upon a scaffold, where she heard the sentence of excommunication read out. Almost immediately she was forced by two sergeants to come down from the platform, and was hurried off to execution. Afterwards there were numerous testimonies about what Jeanne was alleged to have said on the morning of her death: these agreed that she had asserted that a previous story she had told about an angel offering Charles the crown was untrue, and that she herself was the angel; and she is supposed to have cried out that her voices had deceived her.

In compressing the events of six days into six pages, Shaw has undoubtedly heightened the conflict of his scene, both external and internal, and triumphantly raised his play to a stunning climax. Yet whatever dramatic point was successfully made, it is again legitimate to ask, as so many of his critics have, whether or not Shaw at this point falsified the character of his heroine. A careful comparison between fact and fiction reveals instead the brilliance with which Shaw managed to preserve not only the words of Jeanne (as translated by Murray), but also the attitude of mind of the saint.

It was on Thursday, 24 May, we are told, that Jeanne interrupted the reading of the sentence by saying that she would hold all that the Church ordained and all that the judges wished to say and decree. Why did she do this? Murray believed that probably Erard and Loyseleur "were trying to induce Jeanne to recant and sign the schedule, and that her abjuration was the result of their endeavours, not of the Bishop's."[27] Accordingly, Shaw makes Joan yield to the persuasions of Ladvenu:

> Joan [despairing] Oh you are saying what I have said to myself in my fear and my little faith. But it is true: it is true: they have deceived me. I know now that I shall not be delivered and that you will let the English do me to death. Well, they shall not have that satisfaction. I have been mocked by devils: my faith is broken. I have dared and dared; but only a fool will walk into a fire: God, who gave me my commonsense, cannot will me to do that.[28] (fols. 53–54)

There is no warrant in Shaw's source for the jubilation of Brother Martin Ladvenu, or the heartfelt "Amen!" of Cauchon. But the next incidents are faithful reproductions of what happened. We are told that Maître Guillaume Erard asked that the schedule be read to her, and that she be requested to sign it.[29] Jeanne answered that she did not know how to sign. In the same way, Shaw makes Cauchon tell Joan that she must sign a solemn recantation of her heresy.

> Joan = Sign? That means to write my name. But I cannot write.

The recantation itself in Shaw's play is based closely upon that to be found in Murray on pages 130–32. Although it is considerably shortened, it follows exactly the wording of the original with two minor alterations: Shaw changes the phrase "against all the modesty of the feminine sex" to "against all the duties which have made my sex especially acceptable to God" (which last two words were later altered to "in heaven"); and he omits the promise that she will never return to her errors.

Following her reading, Joan has her name written for her and then makes her mark, as is reported on page 173 of Murray, where Erard is alleged to have said to her, "You shall abjure at once, or you shall be burned." And, indeed, before she left the square, she abjured,

> and made a cross with a pen which I handed to her.

According to Mark Twain, though Loyseleur praised her for having done well (an irony that perhaps Shaw borrowed for Ladvenu) "she was still dreamy, she hardly heard."[30] The listlessness of Joan captured in Shaw's stage direction is precisely the mood evoked by Mark Twain.

The Inquisitor's declaration that Joan is now "set free" from the danger of excommunication is ironic in view of the sentence of life imprisonment that he is about to impose; and this irony, too, Shaw found in Murray's translation of the original documents: "We declare thee set free . . . from the bonds of excommunications," runs the sentence,

> But because thou hast sinned rashly against God and Holy Church, We condemn thee, finally, definitely, and for salutary penance, saving Our grace and moderation, to perpetual imprisonment, with the bread of sorrow and the water of affliction, in order that thou mayest bewail thy faults, and that thou mayest no more commit [acts] which thou shalt have to bewail hereafter.[31]

Shaw's sentence, which is almost identical in wording, achieves greater force by leaving the phrase "perpetual imprisonment" to the end. Some of the play's early critics complained of Shaw's unhistoric handling of Joan's relapse.[32] In Shaw's play it is caused by the fear of life imprisonment, which is the only alternative to the ultimate penalty offered by the court. J. Percy Smith attributes this to Shaw's own hatred of imprisonment: "His passion for freedom was . . . deep. He never lost his hatred of enforced restraint, whether of men or animals, and imprisonment seemed to him the supreme cruelty, far worse than death. In *Saint Joan*, it is the threat of solitary confinement that settles the Maid's mind for martyrdom."[33] There is truth in this; but Shaw is still basing his play upon original documents. To begin with, according to the evidence of Maître Guillaume Delachambre, Joan's decision to abjure was made on the understanding that she would be released:

Maître Guillaume Erard decided her by saying that, if she did what he advised her, she would be delivered from prison. She abjured on this condition and no other, and immediately read a small schedule containing six or seven lines on a piece of paper folded in two. I was so near her that, in all truth, I could see the lines and their form.[34]

Moreover, at the time of her abjuration, Jeanne is alleged to have said: "I would rather do penance once for all—that is die—than endure any longer the suffering of a prison.[35] In short, having eliminated the interval from 24 to 28 May before Jeanne's recantation, Shaw still seeks to sum up her feelings after those four days in prison, when the appalling treatment she received after her recantation must have been enough to make her realize that as soon as her confession, be it of fraud or deviltry, was made known to the world, in addition to the imprisonment, she could only become the butt of general scorn, rejected by her family and reviled by the very people who had formerly revered her. In the light of these facts, Shaw the dramatist decided to make his protagonist behave as she did in the courtroom to employ the dramatic power both of compression of events and of sudden peripety.

Another prevailing criticism about Joan's relapse in Shaw's play concerns not its matter, but its manner. The long speech in which she repudiates the "mercy" of the court, rejects the notion of perpetual imprisonment and calls for the fire, has been criticized as fake poetic and sentimental. No doubt this speech was a contributory factor to R. Ellis Roberts' complaint in his review of the first English performance of *Saint Joan*. Roberts, in his evocation of the Victorian womanhood of Ruskin and Tennyson, makes the fatal accusation that Shaw sentimentalizes his heroine, suggesting, however, that the relapse speech is the only moment of contrived pathos in Shaw's play, and questions whether Shaw stumbled over it.

The original manuscript tells us little beyond the fact that since this speech has fewer corrections than any other of comparable length in the play, Shaw was presumably satisfied with it, and took full responsibility for it, since it is practically the only speech in the scene that does not have its origin in Jeanne's actual words. Yet, on examination, although perhaps it lacks the poetry of Joan's speech at the end of Scene V, she is given some fine fighting lines. It is only the descriptive elements that smack of undue convention: "the sight of the fields and flowers," "the wind in the trees," "the larks in the sunshine," and "the young lambs crying through the healthy frost." Although here Shaw may be giving us what Desmond MacCarthy called, in another context, "the tokens of an orator not the images of a poet,"[36] one notes in his mention of the "larks" that he retains by implication his image of the caged bird, perhaps reinforced by his reading of Southey:

> I remember as her corse
> Went to the grave, there was a lark sprung up
> And, soaring in the sunshine, caroll'd loud
> A joyful song; and in mine heart I thought
> That of the multitude of beings, man
> Alone was wretched.[37]

A sensible defence of Joan's speech is made by John Rosselli, who says:

> On paper it is open to criticism. But in the theatre it works, because if the
> scene has been allowed to play itself . . . the audience by that time no longer
> takes in the language as language, but leaps straight to the sense that informs
> the language; and the sense here comes over as a true cry for freedom. What
> the analytical critics forget is that in the theatre the effect is cumulative, the
> moment of transfiguration if it comes, depends not on itself but on the total
> situation as the preceding action has built it up.[38]

Rosselli is, of course, correct: we have followed Joan's career through four acts,
and the moment is climactic. But even in its immediate context the speech is
defensible: it is not, after all, to be spoken as by one of Tennyson's heroines. It
opens with the statement "They [meaning her voices] told me you were fools";
and it ends with "I know that your counsel is of the devil, and that mine is of
God": both statements calculated to arouse the fury of the assembled priests and
jurors. Indeed, in revision, Shaw added after the word "fools" the stage direction
"The word gives great offence," and after her final sentence, again in revision, the
assessors explode, "Blasphemy! blasphemy! She is possessed." It is worth remarking at this point that all the assessors' interruptions are additions to the script,
made during his revision in Ireland, none appearing in the original shorthand. By
sandwiching the descriptive portion of Joan's speech between two insults calculated to create uproar in the court, Shaw insures a groundswell of indignant noise
rising to a climax over which Joan must actually shout her final lines.

This powerful moment is continued by D'Estivet, shouting above the din that
Joan is a relapsed heretic, then taken up by the Chaplain (originally it said "shouting") telling the Executioner to light the fire, and take Joan to the stake; this gives
way to Joan's final speech of only three lines, in which, like Christ Himself, she
announces that her kingdom is not of this world. The soldiers seize her; and then
all noise suddenly ceases, as Cauchon rises and says "Not yet." The stage direction at this point is "There is a dead silence."

The sentence, which is antiphonally intoned by Cauchon and the Inquisitor, is
condensed from Murray, pages 143–44. After the sentence is read, we have the

Chaplain crying, "Into the fire with the witch," and according to the stage direction he rushes at her, and helps the soldiers to push her out.[39] Shaw's picture of this scene was no doubt remembered from the deposition of Laurence Guesdon, Burgher of Rouen, who was at the final sermon at the old marketplace:[40]

> The sentence by which Jeanne was handed over to the civil authorities was read; and, as soon as it was pronounced—at once, without any interval of handing her over to the Bailly, without more ado, and before either the Bailly or myself, whose office it was, had given sentence,—the executioner seized her and took her to the place where the stake was already prepared: and she was burned. And this I hold was not a right proceeding: for soon after, a malefactor named George Folenfont was in like manner handed over, by sentence, from the ecclesiastical to the civil authorities; and, after the sentence, the said George was conducted to the Cohue[41] and there condemned by the secular justice, instead of being immediately conducted to execution.

Accordingly, Shaw makes Cauchon protest:

> No, no: this is irregular. The representatives of the secular arm should be here to receive her from us.

At this point, while the faggots are crackling in the market place, the Inquisitor reveals a darker side to his character; pointing out to Cauchon the advantages that might accrue to them from allowing the English to put themselves in the wrong. This is something of a shock, coming from the mild and apparently just cleric whom we have seen in the earlier part of this scene. Shaw himself seems to have faltered a little, giving to Cauchon originally the line "That man is the most incorrigible fool,"[42] and Cauchon's later line "These English are impossible: they will thrust her straight into the fire" to the Inquisitor, whose name is later crossed out in the original shorthand. However, Shaw makes the point shortly that the Inquisitor, though he regrets the necessity for such burnings, has become accustomed to them. It is, he admits, a terrible thing

> to see a young and innocent creature crushed between these mighty forces, the Church and the Law.
> Cauchon = You call her innocent!
> The Inquisitor = Oh, quite innocent. What does she know of the Church and the Law? She did not understand a word we were saying. It is the ignorant who suffer, not the guilty. Come or we shall be late for the end.[43] (fol. 57)

Cauchon's first response to this speech was:

> Cauchon [going with him] I shall not be sorry if they have (sic): I am not so accustomed as you. I hope they will make short work of it, and that she will not scream.

No doubt Shaw's desire to make the execution as graphic as possible without actually putting it on the stage gave way to his dramatic instinct, which was to give the Bishop a brief, realistic response. There is more impact in such understatement.

As Cauchon and the Inquisitor leave, Warwick enters, and there is a short, almost hostile exchange between the Bishop and the English Earl, to emphasize the difference in the victories they have achieved. Warwick is then left alone on the stage; and in the first draft he rings a bell on the table, in an attempt to attract the attention of his page, Brian. Perhaps with the opening of the as yet unwritten Epilogue in mind, and Charles's similar use of the rattle, Shaw excluded this stage direction at a later date, and simply made Warwick call in the silence. It is significant that his page does not come: everybody, including the child, has gone to witness the burning.

The scene that follows is another excellent example of the way in which Shaw adapts history to his own dramatic purposes without falsifying the facts. At least three witnesses of the execution of Jeanne d'Arc collapsed, overcome with feelings of guilt and remorse. The first was the executioner himself, who, according to the eyewitness testimony of Brother Ysambard de la Pierre, "Immediately after the execution...came to me and to my companion, Brother Martin Ladvenu, stricken and moved with a marvellous repentance and terrible contrition, quite desperate and fearing never to obtain pardon and indulgence from God for what he had done to this holy woman."[44] Later, this same witness made the following addition to his evidence:

> On this same occasion, the Bishop of Beauvais wept. A certain Englishman, a soldier, who hated her greatly, had sworn to bring a faggot for the stake. When he did so, and heard Jeanne calling on the name of Jesus in her last moments, he was stupefied, and, as it were in an ecstasy at the spectacle: his companions took him and led him away to a neighbouring tavern. After refreshment, he revived. In the afternoon, the same Englishman confessed, in my presence, to a brother of the Order of St. Dominic, that he had gravely erred, and that he repented of what he had done against Jeanne. He held her to be a good woman, for he had seen the spirit departing from her, as it were a white dove, going away from France.

In the afternoon of the same day, the executioner came to the Convent of the Dominicans, saying to them and to Brother Martin Ladvenu, that he feared he was damned because he had burned a saint.

This testimony is corroborated by a citizen of Rouen, Maître Pierre Cusquel, who on 9 May 1452, stated: "Maître Jean Tressart, when he returned from the execution, groaning and weeping sadly, lamented to me what he had seen at this place, saying to me: 'We are all lost; we have burnt a Saint'; adding, that he believed her soul was in the hands of God because, when she was in the midst of the flames, she constantly called on the name of the Lord Jesus." In Shaw's play, while Warwick stands in the deserted courtroom, the unearthly silence is broken by the sound of someone "frantically howling and sobbing." It is the Chaplain, de Stogumber, returning from the execution. In some sense, therefore, he is able to represent both the contrition of the clergy (we never see Cauchon in this scene again) and the perfidy of the British — particularly of those with such an implacable hatred of Joan. De Stogumber would have been delighted to bring a faggot to the fire that burned her.

His violent reversal of role, much more than the change that came over the Inquisitor, is a shock to the sensibilities of the audience. It is dramatically highly effective, too, for the reason given by J. I. M. Stewart in *Eight Modern Writers*, who speaks of Shaw's "new tact" in the use of laughter, citing both the halo effect on de Baudricourt at the end of Scene I, and the fact that John de Stogumber, who has been a buffoon all along, is used in serious vein at the end of the Trial Scene.

De Stogumber's speech when he enters is brief but effective; though its effectiveness was only achieved at the cost of some correction. The alterations involve a simple tightening of the dialogue by omission of unnecessary phrases. Since the page bearing this speech is among the few sheets of typescript that were not destroyed, it is easier than usual to follow Shaw's corrections, which bring the speech back from its original unpunctuated breathless state (presumably intended to represent the Chaplain's incoherence) to Shaw's own rhetorically powerful style. The dashes of the original are replaced by the familiar colons and semi-colons, and the address to Christ is changed from "you" to "Thee." This necessitated the removal of an ugly sentence, which had originally been "And you delivered her by death." Its alteration to "Thou deliveredst her by death" was found to be awkward to pronounce, and it was dropped as part of the tightening process.

Warwick calms the Chaplain down, but the latter continues, albeit more quietly, to describe — for us as well as for Warwick — the scene of Joan's execution:

She asked for a cross. A soldier gave her two sticks tied together. Thank God he was an Englishman.

In his "Note by the Author," in the program of the New Theatre, Shaw stated that "the English soldier represents a cherished tradition if not an authentic fact," and in a letter to the editor of the *Spectator* on 21 February 1925, he felt moved to apologize for the soldier, saying, "The tradition that a common English soldier tied two sticks together and gave them to her, and that she died with that cross in her bosom, has always seemed to me so heroic, and so redemptive of the otherwise unrelieved ferocity of our share in the tragedy, that I innocently supposed my feeling about it to be a general possession." It is difficult to see why Shaw is so defensive: according to the eyewitness testimony of Maître Jean Massieu the incident actually did occur. Although, admittedly, there is no mention of the person being a soldier, since he was English and in the market square at Rouen at the time, it seems highly likely that that was his profession:

> When she was given over by the Church, I was still with her; and with great devotion she asked to have a Cross: and, hearing this, an Englishman who was there present, made a little cross of wood with the ends of a stick, which he gave her, and devoutly she received and kissed it, making piteous lamentations and acknowledgements to God, Our Redeemer, Who had suffered on the Cross for our redemption, of Whose Cross she had the sign and symbol; and she put the said Cross in her bosom, between her person and her clothing.[45]

Shaw's use of the same phrase "in her bosom" might suggest that he was remembering his source even though, in his "Note," he had cast doubt on its factual truth.

Shaw makes de Stogumber's mention of the charity of the English soldier the occasion for a further revelation of Warwick's coldness of character:

> I must see that the priests do not get hold of him: I will have no inquisitioning of *my* soldiers. (fol. 58)

Later, Shaw strengthened this to:

> The fool! they will burn him too if the priests get hold of him.

This comment is juxtaposed with the Chaplain's continuing picture of the horror of the execution:

> Some of the people laughed at her. They would have laughed at Christ. They were French people, my lord: I know they were French.

This again comes from an eyewitness account, this time of Maître Guillaume Delachambre; but it is interesting to note the way in which Shaw has adapted it to his character, and even walked successfully the fine line between comedy and pathos by fusing together de Stogumber's nationalism and his dementia.

Brother Martin's dramatic entrance, carrying the cross from a local church, puts a stop to any further talk from the Chaplain. He gravely explains that he took the cross from the church so that Joan might see it to the last. This, in fact, did happen, though the person who held it up that she might see it was Brother Ysambard de la Pierre, Ladvenu's companion. Such a timely appearance on stage of this reminder of Christ's passion, however, is dramatically appropriate both to reinforce the parallel with Jesus' martyrdom, and to foreshadow Joan's symbolic resurrection in the Epilogue. Again following the facts, Shaw, through Brother Martin, reports the remarkable selflessness of Jeanne:

> But when she saw that if I held it up I should be burnt myself she warned me to get down and save myself.

Shaw's comment on this appears in the next sentence:

> My lord: a girl who could think of another's danger in such a moment was not inspired by the devil.

It was widely reported that Jeanne's last words were "Jesus! Jesus!" With memories of the visionary Joan, Shaw symbolizes her last moments thus:

> When I had to spring down and snatch the cross from her sight, she looked up to heaven. And I do not believe that the heavens were empty. I firmly believe that her Savior appeared to her in His tenderest glory. She called on Him and died.

Warwick remains tenaciously unmoved and expedient, merely complaining that such behaviour will have a bad effect on the people.

> Ladvenu = It had, my lord, on some of them. I heard laughter. Forgive me for saying that I hope and believe it was English laughter.

Ladvenu is correct in his belief, according to the evidence, which, however, since it is French evidence, could hardly be impartial on the matter. The comment is the signal for the wild exit of the Chaplain, who, hearing in it his own shame again, runs from the room crying that he should be tortured and burned, and that he will pray among her ashes. Warwick sends Brother Martin after him, fearing that de Stogumber, having likened himself to Judas, will seek the same end, and this clears the stage for a final confrontation with a third witness of Joan's execution: the Executioner himself. Shaw presents him as differently as possible from the abject figure who appears in the various depositions in Murray, where he is seen as pleading for mercy for having burnt a saint. Shaw makes him a solemn, dignified creature, who objects to being addressed by the Earl of Warwick as "fellow." He identifies himself as the Master Executioner of Rouen. It is, he says, a highly skilled trade. Shaw later changed the word "trade" to "mystery" thus intensifying our awareness that we are in the presence of the agent, if not the angel, of death. Warwick certainly seems somewhat chastened by the reflection, and promises that the Executioner will not lose anything by having no relics to sell.

> I have your word, have I, that nothing remains, not a hair, not a nail, not a bone?[46] (fol. 59)

The Executioner's reply is, perhaps, something of a shock to twentieth-century ears:

> Her heart would not burn, sir, but everything that was left is at the bottom of the river.[47]

In this we are seeing the beginning of the legend that was to surround the Maid's name for five hundred years, but Shaw is still basing his work firmly upon fact as reported in Murray. For when the real executioner came desperately before Brother Martin and Ysambard de la Pierre craving forgiveness, he did indeed affirm that,

> notwithstanding the oil, the sulphur, and the charcoal which he had applied to the entrails and heart of the said Jeanne, in no way had he been able to burn them up, nor reduce to cinders either the entrails or the heart, at which he was much astonished, as a most evident miracle.[48]

Somehow, the quiet dignity, and total lack of astonishment of Shaw's Executioner, makes his recital of this last "miracle" all the more powerful, adding, perhaps, an air of inevitability, which raises to a symbolic level the closing moments of this scene. It is enough for even the pragmatic Warwick to doubt whether the world has heard the last of Joan of Arc.

5

The Memory and the Salvation

When Shaw's play first appeared, the Epilogue created more critical dissension than all the other scenes put together. Jack Crawford of the *Drama* stated: "If I were to find something too obvious in the play, I should choose the epilogue, for I believed all Mr. Shaw wanted me to believe without its being retold me once more."[1] A more extreme view was expressed by J. L. Kimball, who, a year later described the Epilogue as "wanton destruction" and a "perfectly appalling" ending to the play.[2] On the other hand, for R. Ellis Roberts, the Epilogue was "easily the most successful part of the play."[3] And this opinion was seconded by Reginald Owen, for whom the Epilogue was "the finishing touch to a work of great genius."[4] The objectors may have been influenced by the extreme length of the play in performance, a saturation point having been reached by the end of the Trial Scene; or, as Helen MacAfee suggested, the problem may have been one of adjusting to the more characteristic mood of the Epilogue, "with all its clownish pranks," after the power and drama of Joan's trial.[5] Some, however, clearly felt the need for a change of mood: "There has been much discussion of the dramatic propriety of Mr. Shaw's epilogue, but it has the excuse of being thoroughly entertaining."[6]

The subsequent half century has seen little diminution of the debate. E. J. West describes the Epilogue as "originally much deprecated and now accepted but almost always made the subject of some apology by the critics."[7] And A. N. Kaul sums up the case for the opposition:

> . . . it is unfortunate that Shaw thought it necessary to underline the triumphant quality of Joan's tale, its glorious ending by writing an Epilogue, which he not only wrote but defended against all objections. With its fantasy tableaux, its flip jokes, its common soldiers (on a day's parole from Hell) railing against "kings and captains and bishops" and telling Joan that she has "as good a right to your notions as they have to theirs"—even with Joan's famous last cry: "How long, O Lord, how long?"—the Epilogue mostly brings back the Shaw so admirably absent from the play itself.[8]

"When critics disagree," said Oscar Wilde, "the artist is in accord with himself." And Shaw had no doubts as to what he was doing. He gives his raison d'être for the scene in his "Note by the Author" as follows: "Without it the play would be only a sensational tale of a girl who was burnt, leaving spectators plunged in horror, despairing of humanity."[9] The Epilogue certainly adds an eternal perspective to what have hitherto been considerations political and national, fettered by a temporal framework. As I have suggested, that a "resurrection" would follow the burning is surely signalled by the final events of the previous scene; thus, in the Epilogue, Shaw is able to reveal the Life Force making use of suffering and death to further its positive purposes. And this reminds us that not only is the Epilogue central to Shaw's drama, but that it might have been *l'idée mère* for the whole play, lurking in his subconscious for ten years; for in a letter to Mrs. Patrick Campbell (8 September 1913)[10] Shaw had envisaged his Joan play in terms of judgement after Joan's death, and his first suggestion for a setting had been the streets of heaven.

The Epilogue, however, is not set in heaven, although, as we shall see, it possesses incorporeal elements about it which are ultimately vital to Shaw's thesis. Shaw began writing it on 6 August 1923, and drew a full picture of his scene:

> The king's bedchamber in the royal chateau of ----. The bed is raised on a dais of two steps; and the head has a canopy with the royal arms embroidered. The bed is not a four poster: except for the canopy there is nothing to distinguish it from a broad settee with bedclothes and a valance, the view of its occupant from the foot and sides being quite unobstructed. At present its huge down pillows are being pressed by King Charles the Seventh, who is reading in bed, or rather looking at the pictures in the ------ -------'s Boccaccio, with his knees doubled up to make a reading desk. Tall candles of painted wax are in standard candlesticks on both sides. The wall beside the bed is pierced by a tall lancet window on Charles's right, opening to within a foot of the floor. The door is in the side wall, also to his right, but in front of him near the corner farthest from him. There is a large watchman's rattle handsomely designed and gaily painted, in the bed close to Charles's hand.
>
> Charles turns a leaf and chuckles appreciatively at the new picture revealed. A clock strikes the quarter. Charles shuts the book with a clap; throws it aside; snatches up the rattle and whirls it energetically, making a deafening noise. Ladvenu enters. Charles springs out of bed on the farther side from the newcomer. (fol. 60)

This does not differ markedly from the final version of 1924, which adds only the "painted curtains" whose "yellow and red ... is somewhat flamelike when the folds breathe in the wind," and which substracts the "appreciative" chuckle at the picture from de Fouquet's illustrated *Decameron*.

On his entrance, Ladvenu propounds a paradox: at the trial which sent a saint to the stake the truth was told and law was observed; at the inquiry he has just come from there was shameless perjury and calumny of the dead, and yet out of it "the truth is set in the noonday sun on the hilltop." Charles is unmoved:

> If a fair trial put the Maid in the wrong and an unfair one has put her in the right, honors are easy between the two. (fol. 61)

But the paradox of the two trials is crucial. We are meant to be reminded of an earlier juxtaposition of truth and falsehood. A miracle, asserted the Archbishop in Scene II, is an event which creates faith:

> Miracles are not frauds because they are often—I do not say always—very simple and innocent contrivances by which the priest fortifies the faith of his flock. (fol. 15)

In these events we are made to feel something of the "mystic pragmatism," as it has been called, of Shaw. The injustice of the death of Christ led to the triumph of his resurrection; in a sense we owe Christianity to the perfidy of Judas. The divine scheme is mysterious: the Life Force induces men to perform certain deeds for reasons beyond their understanding, but which ultimately further its purposes. Blanco Posnet steals a horse to leave town. He gives it to the mother of a sick child, and is consequently caught and arrested. But the innocent child dies; and the guilty Blanco is set at liberty. Such paradoxes baffle the shade of Cauchon, who is "still dreaming of justice."

> The earth rocks beneath the feet of men and spirits alike when the innocent are slain in the name of right and their wrongs are undone by slandering the pure of heart.

But Joan sees clearly:

> Well, well, Peter, men will be the better for remembering me; and they would not remember me so well if you had not burned me. (fol. 63)

And de Stogumber brings further proof. He was saved by his own cruelty! As Joan expresses it:

> Well, if I saved all that you would have been cruel to if you had not been cruel to me I did not burn altogether in vain. (fol. 65)

There is great significance, then, in the line,

> Must then a Christ perish in torment in every generation to save those that
> have no imagination?[11] (fol. 65)

Originally Shaw gave this line to Joan; but must have realized that it sorted ill
with her understanding, and so gave it, more appropriately, to Cauchon. However, lest we be simple-minded enough to think that it is Judas and Cauchon who
are to be thanked, Joan has one more word to say on the subject. When Warwick,
the secular pragmatist, says:

> Still, when they make you a saint, as they most certainly ought to, you will
> owe your halo to me, just as this lucky monarch owes his crown to you. (fol.
> 66)

Joan turns from him with the words,

> I owe nothing to any man: I owe everything to the spirit of God that was
> within me.

As can be seen by comparing the manuscript quotations above with what they
became in the printed version, the alterations in this scene are fairly slight. Since
it was written in Ireland, where Shaw did not have access to all his books, spaces
are occasionally left for factual addition: "Leave the rest of the page to fill in this,"
writes Shaw when Ladvenu arrives to explain the official terms of Joan's rehabilitation; and "Leave a short blank for particulars," is Shaw's further injunction to
Blanche Patch when Charles is telling Joan how his fighting days have been since
her departure. In the same way Dunois is equally vague as he tells Joan how he
has beaten the goddams for her:

> Aye: I beat them for you at   : I beat them for you at   : I made a
> clean sweep in the end: they had to go. (fol. 63)

In addition to the few pieces that remained to be added during revision, Shaw
saw fit to remove a speech here and there. These are few in number, and not
highly significant; but one lost exchange between Joan and Warwick is worth
recording: Warwick is accounting for the expulsion of the English from France,
and admits that the burning of Joan was a mistake, as it fired the populace to
national enthusiasm:

> The consequence of it was that this extremely second rate king, and this not
> very extraordinary captain—no abler at any rate than our Henry the Fifth or

the Black Prince, carried us out of France almost before your venerated ashes were cold. At Crecy, Poitiers, Agincourt, we were irresistible. What made the difference?

Dunois = I made the difference. But she made the difference to me.

Joan = Thou didst not do it singlehanded, Jack. I tell thee again that the yeomen of England in their leather jerkins won all those battles against the fops from the tilting yards of France in their fine armour; but when the Frenchmen from the fields and farms took the matter up to put the English back where God put them, thou hadst but to plan the victory for them to win it. (fol. 66)

The remaining alterations are, as in the earlier scenes, rhetorical. Shaw raises his play to a climax by a superb selection of words. Nowhere is this more evident than in the antiphonal chorus of praise for Joan by the other characters. One by one they kneel, and pronounce their words of praise, which, in rhythm and spirit, echo the Beatitudes of the third chapter of St. Matthew's gospel. Shaw worked hard to improve each speech poetically:

British Library Add. MSS. 45923, fols. 67–68	*Saint Joan* (London: Constable & Co., 1924)
Cauchon [kneeling] The girls in the field praise thee; for there is nothing between them and the skies.	[*kneeling to her*] The girls in the field praise thee; for thou hast raised their eyes; and they see that there is nothing between them and heaven.
Dunois [kneeling] The soldiers in the trench praise thee, because thou art a shield between them and hell.	[*kneeling to her*] The dying soldiers praise thee, because thou art a shield of glory between them and the judgment.
The Archbishop [appearing and kneeling] The princes of the Church praise thee because thou hast redeemed the worship they betrayed.	[*kneeling to her*] The princes of the Church praise thee, because thou hast redeemed the faith their worldlinesses have dragged through the mire.
Warwick = The rulers and their counsellors praise thee because thou gavest back to them the heritage they wasted.	[*kneeling to her*] The cunning counsellors praise thee, because thou hast cut the knots in which they have tied their own souls.
De Stogumber = The old men on their deathbed praise thee because their sins against thee have turned into blessings.	[*kneeling to her*] The foolish old men on their deathbeds praise thee, because their sins against thee are turned into blessings.
The Inquisitor [appearing and kneeling] The blinded judges praise thee	[*kneeling to her*] The judges in the blindness and bondage of the law

because thou hast opened their eyes and rebuked their presumption.

The Soldier = The wicked out of hell praise thee because thou hast shewn that the fire that is not quenched is a holy fire.

The Executioner [kneeling] The tormentors and the executioners praise thee because thou hast shewn that their hands are guiltless of the death of the soul.

Charles [kneelings] (sic) The cowards and the weaklings praise thee, because thou hast lifted the load of terror from them.

praise thee, because thou hast vindicated the vision and the freedom of the living soul.

[*kneeling to her*] The wicked out of hell praise thee, because thou hast shewn that the fire that is not quenched is a holy fire.

[*kneeling to her*] The tormentors and executioners praise thee, because thou hast shewn that their hands are guiltless of the death of the soul.

[*kneeling to her*] The unpretending praise thee, because thou hast taken upon thyself the heroic burdens that are too heavy for them.

The alterations are interesting. In the original version, only the French kneel to Joan; and one notices that the Archbishop and the Inquisitor have to "appear" before they can kneel, no provision for their arrival on stage having been made yet. The clumsiness of this Shaw was to smooth away by the simple addition of a stage direction, bringing the Archbishop and the Inquisitor into view as the vision of Rheims Cathedral fades. In the second version, all the characters kneel to the saint and their speeches take on a greater rhetorical resonance. The style becomes openly biblical, and this paves the way for Joan's response to this chorus of praise:

Woe unto me when all men praise me!

which is clearly an echo of St. Luke, vi, verse 26:

Woe unto you when all men shall speak well of you!

Joan's offer, in her newly powerful sainthood, to return to them is refused: the lights go out, and the kneeling worshippers spring to their feet in consternation.[12] Joan's question (added to the original), "Must I burn again?" is an echo of Cauchon's earlier thought that a Christ must perish in torment in every age to save those who have no imagination.

This idea of the redemptive power of the imagination is not only the climactic statement of the Epilogue, it is the clue to Shaw's relationship with his heroine, and a key to the dramatic statement of the entire play. Even in Scene I, when quizzed by Robert de Baudricourt about her visions, Joan explains:

Joan = No: it is quite different. I cannot tell you: you must not talk to me about my voices.

Robert = Oh! Voices! How do you know the voices are not all your imagination?

Joan = But they *are* all my imagination. That is how the will of God comes to us. (fol. 7)

There was an immediate critical outcry at this apparent rationalization.[13] Loudest of all the critics was J. M. Robertson, who tried to ridicule Shaw's line here, saying: "By his own account he uses dramatic imagination to write his plays. Then we have this pleasing dilemma. Either his mental processes are what he declared Joan's voices to have been, hallucinations, or Jeanne did not actually hear and see the voices and visions she alleged."[14] The attempted ridicule is a failure, because Robertson has accidentally hit on a truth. Shaw, as a matter of fact, did believe that his mental processes in playwriting produced Joan-like hallucinations. In fact, as William Searle points out,[15] long before writing *Saint Joan*, he had been interested in how and why the imagination dramatizes its intuitions, and had found the answer in his experience as a playwright:

I am not governed by principles; I am inspired, how or why I cannot explain, because I do not know, but inspiration it must be; for it comes to me without any reference to my own ends or interests.

I find myself possessed of a theme in the following manner. I am pushed by a natural need to set to work to write down the conversations that come into my head unaccountably. At first I hardly know the speakers, and cannot find names for them. Then they become more and more familiar, and I learn their names. Finally I come to know them very well, and discover what it is they are driving at, and why they have said and done the things I have been moved to set down.

This is not being guided by principles: it is hallucination; and sane hallucination is what we call play or drama.[16]

As Searle explains, Shaw's use of the word "inspiration" in this passage suggests that a creative effort of the imagination can come to us from the Life Force; the phrase "a natural need," which it answers, is clearly biological; and the fact that it is a "superpersonal" rather than a private need, suggests that it must be a need of evolution. Thus, concludes Searle, the Life Force in which Shaw believed (like the God of Christianity, in which he did not believe) is able to enlighten the understanding of its agents without the aid of their physical senses.

Further, although Shaw's view that Joan's voices were analogous to the creations of imaginative writers (including his own) is not an original one (Michelet mentions it), Shaw's Butlerian Vitalism allowed him to go much further than Michelet in defining the analogy between hallucination and inspiration. It allowed him to derive from the Romantic doctrine of inspiration (which he shared with Michelet) an aesthetic which virtually identifies artistic creation with organic process. And, finally, since the artist's methods are the same as nature's, Shaw adds that they may normally be expected to *anticipate* the findings of the scientist; which is why Joan replies to Dunois, after he remarks that he would think Joan a bit cracked if she did not give him sensible reasons for what she does:

> Well, I have to find reasons for you, because you do not believe in my voices. But the voices come first; and I find the reasons after: whatever you may choose to believe.

But of course, the imagination can be a dangerous master: the delusions of the mentally infirm are hardly a reliable guide to conduct! Shaw, however, had already tackled that problem, with the aid of Schopenhauer, and in 1914, in the Preface to *Misalliance* he had, like Schopenhauer, distinguished between two kinds of imagination. The wise man, he explains, knows that imagination is not only a means of pleasing himself and beguiling tedious hours with romances and fairy tales and fools' paradises "but also a means of foreseeing and being prepared for realities as yet unexperienced, and of testing the feasibility of serious Utopias."

The fullest expression of this in Shaw's work is to be found in *Back to Methuselah*, where he suggests that since there is no such thing as the future until it is the present, the "realistic imagination necessarily plays a vital role in all acts of creativity and invention." In that metabiological pentateuch it is the serpent in the Garden of Eden who is the spokesman—or rather spokeswoman—for this doctrine.[17] She explains creation to Eve:

> Before a thing is created, it must first be desired; and since it does not yet exist, the imagination alone is capable of making it an object of desire. You imagine what you desire: you will what you imagine; and at last you create what you will...

She thus implies that nature's methods of creation are the same as those of poets; which is why Shaw says in his Preface: "the figure that Joan recognized as St Catherine was not really St Catherine, but the dramatization by Joan's imagination of that pressure upon her of the driving force that is behind evolution, which I have just called the evolutionary appetite."[18]

Now the interesting thing in *Saint Joan* is the way in which Shaw makes the everyday imagination of his characters symbolize different degrees of the creative imagination. The response of the various characters to Joan is determined by their imaginative faculty. The first believer in her, de Poulengy, is described as "dreamily absentminded."[19] The Dauphin boasts that he can read, but is content to leaf through the illustrations in his Boccaccio. Warwick admires the aesthetic beauty of books, but deplores the increasing tendency to regard them as simply vehicles of information. Beauty feeds the imagination; and a well-fed imagination enables one to make and hold in one's mind images for absent things. La Trémouille's comment on Pythagoras is instructive here: "Who the deuce was Pythagoras?" he asks. The Archbishop explains:

A sage who held that the earth is round, and that it moves round the sun . . .

to which la Trémouille replies:

What an utter fool! Couldn't he use his eyes?

Dunois is a person of some imagination—admittedly not a great deal. His versifying is about as bad as that of the anonymous author of the "Ode to Hanky"; and his love of the beauty of the kingfishers is not conclusive; but his threat when his page wants to trap a kingfisher:

Let me catch you trying to trap them, and I will put you in the iron cage for a month to teach you what a cage feels like . . .

reveals that, Dunois, unlike de Stogumber, is at least capable of imagining the suffering such an action would bring about. Indeed, de Stogumber is the play's most fearful example of brute understanding. He has no imagination at all, receiving the highly coloured and largely fictitious accounts of Joan's actions as witchcraft: he is presented as a literalist: damning proof that the English are strangely blunt in the mind. Warwick, in Scene IV, excuses his own lack of imagination in "taking the burning of this poor girl too lightly":

When one has seen whole countrysides burnt over and over again as mere items of military routine, one has to grow a very thick skin. Otherwise one might go mad: at all events, I should . . .

This of course is the fate of de Stogumber, who, like Lady Macbeth, is not tormented before the deed because he has insufficient imagination to conjure up what it might be like, but whose reason is unhinged by the sight of it. In the Trial Scene Joan is surrounded by rationalists. Ironically they are all churchmen. They are as unimaginative and literal as it is possible to be: as, indeed they were in fact. They insist upon "the whole truth." In vain does Joan tell them that God does not allow the whole truth to be told. In other words, there is a limit to rational explanations. "Do what was done last time is thy rule," she says to Courcelles, and neatly describes the lack of evolutionary will possessed by the whole court. Even the Inquisitor, perhaps the most intelligent member of the court, betrays the limitations of theological rationalism in his celebrated defence of religion, law, and order, which is an eminently reasonable argument, but, as William Searle demonstrates,[20] is grounded in reason which proceeds from and is subordinate to the *will*; a reason which can find a dozen reasons for doing what it wants and can argue with equal cogency on both sides of any question. Even in small matters Shaw demonstrates this principle of creative imagination; only, as a matter of fact, the court considered it a very large matter indeed: I am referring to Joan's wearing of men's clothes, which the court described as indecent, unnatural, and abominable. But the accurate reason Joan gives for continuing to dress as a man is "If I were to dress as a woman, the soldiers would think of me as a woman." In other words they, too, deal in appearances, and it is a fairly simple matter to delude them. Naturally, Joan doesn't stand a chance of forwarding creative evolution in a courtroom of people who are facing backwards; so she is sentenced and burned.

Now it becomes clear why Shaw insisted that the Epilogue was essential to his play. Of course, in one sense it is the only part which is his; for there is no source for it except Shaw's imagination. And, appropriately enough, it is also set *in* the imagination of one of the characters! It takes place in the dream of Charles VII. In the dream, Charles and Dunois, who are asleep, meet and talk with Joan and Cauchon, who are dead, and de Stogumber, who is "astray in his wits"; and later with a dead soldier (straight from Hell) and a Gentleman who won't be born for four and half centuries. The factor common to all these people is that they are all "free of the body" as Joan puts it; and thus as free as the imagination to transcend spatial and temporal limitations: they can travel in space from France to England, and in time from the fifteenth to the twentieth century.

It is important for Shaw's purpose to reveal the power of the imagination to form the future: because this is precisely what the will does in the process of creative evolution: it wills into being that which is necessary for the furtherance of the purposes of the Life Force among men. In this sense not only are the happenings of the Epilogue a demonstration of the power of the creative imagination, but the very creation of the play *Saint Joan* is analogous to it. It is, therefore, not only for all the persons of the play, but in a real sense for all of us, that "a Saint must perish in every age to save those who have no imagination." The audience watches sadly, yet with greater understanding, as Joan is rejected a second time in the play, until she is left alone with the sleeping Charles, and the soldier, her "one faithful." It is appropriate that they should be together at the end, these two, the saint and he who held two sticks together and imagined them a cross. Like all imaginative people, he asks questions. In this, he resembles the peasant girl from Lorraine. "What do they all amount to?" he asks rhetorically of the retreating backs of the noblemen and clerics. But the bell strikes, and he is summoned below. And when the "white radiance" descends on Joan, "alone except for the sleeping king hidden in his bedclothes," it is in Shaw's voice that she asks the final question of the play, a question to which our creative imagination in the service of the Life Force must respond:

O God that madest this beautiful earth, when will it be ready to receive Thy saints? How long, O Lord, how long?[21]

6

First Performances

Bernard Shaw's *Saint Joan* was produced for the first time by the Theatre Guild of New York at the Garrick Theatre, on the evening of Friday, 28 December 1923. That it should have been first performed in New York is not surprising: from the time the Theatre Guild presented *Heartbreak House* in 1920 until the production of *The Simpleton of the Unexpected Isles* in 1935, the world premières of all of Shaw's major plays (except *The Apple Cart*) were presented by the Theatre Guild. Of course, Shaw's reputation, which was at that time arguably greater in America than in Europe, went back in the United States to before the turn of the century. In a letter to Archibald Henderson (Shaw's first biographer), James Huneker once claimed the honour of having introduced Bernard Shaw to the American public through his article "A Music Critic's Play"— a review of *Arms and The Man*, which appeared in the *Recorder* early in 1894. Richard Mansfield, who impersonated Bluntschli in that play three years later, directed and acted in the world première of *The Devil's Disciple* at Harmanus Bleecker Hall, Albany, New York. It is said that a performance of *Candida*, given by the Browning Society of Philadelphia, inspired Arnold Daly to produce the same play on 8 December 1903 at the Princess Theatre, New York. It ran for 150 performances, and established Shaw's reputation in the United States twelve months before the Vedrenne/ Barker productions at the Court Theatre in London performed the same service in England. It is, therefore, not surprising to find that the first full-length book about Shaw to appear in any language, *George Bernard Shaw: His Plays*, was written by an American, H. L. Mencken, and published in 1905, just two years after the Daly success; and that Shaw's first official biographer, Archibald Henderson, was also an American.

In 1911, the year that Henderson's first biography of Shaw was published, another American was being introduced to the work of the playwright for the first time. This was Lawrence Langner, later treasurer and production supervisor of the Theatre Guild of New York, who, making his first visit to Britain, participated in a play-reading of Shaw's *Press Cuttings* at the house of a friend. Others who took part were to form, with Langner, the nucleus of the Washington Square Players and produce *Mrs Warren's Profession* at the Comedy Theatre, New York, on 11 March 1918. The play was not a success, but it did not dampen Langner's enthusiasm for Shaw. The Theatre Guild of New York had its first season the following year, producing plays by Jacinto Benavente and by St. John Ervine. Its second season, 1919–20, added dramatists John Masefield, Lillian Sabine, Tolstoy, and Strindberg to the list; and its third season produced the world première of Shaw's *Heartbreak House*, on 10 November 1920.

Langner himself journeyed to England in the winter of 1920/21 to obtain permission to produce a series of Shaw's plays in the United States, and met Shaw for the first time. The "series of plays" which he obtained permission to produce turned out to be *Back to Methuselah*, Shaw's enormously long pentateuch; and the Guild's experience with these five plays, and particularly the objections to their length made by the critics, influenced their negotiating pattern with Shaw over *Saint Joan*, and led to the dispute with him over the length of that play. Langner came to England in the summer of 1922 to negotiate the possibility of making cuts in the script of *Back to Methuselah*, which had started its run on 27 February, and was successful. However, when, on that occasion, he asked if there was any new play in the offing, Mrs. Shaw is alleged to have said that they were not able to find a good subject for one. It was St. John Ervine who, in the summer of 1923, first told Langner that *Saint Joan* was being written. Langner immediately wrote to Shaw stating that the Guild would like to perform it, and hoping that he would let them. And, since *Back to Methuselah* was to be produced in England by the Birmingham Repertory Theatre, Langner wrote to St. John Ervine suggesting that they visit Birmingham together, and he agreed. Meanwhile, Shaw wrote back giving his permission for the Guild to perform his new play, stating: "Saint Joan is finished except for revising and inserting stage business. It's a star play for one woman and about twenty men. Sybil Thorndike is to play it in London."[1] At this juncture, there seems to have been no thought that the New York production would necessarily be the world première. However, Sybil Thorndike who opened at the New Theatre in H. A. Jones's *The Lie*[2] on 13 October, expecting it to run for only a few weeks, found it still going strong after six months; so the Theatre Guild played *Saint Joan* first.[3]

As arranged, Lawrence Langner visited England in 1923 and in October called on the Shaws to hear the dramatist expatiate on his new play. Inevitably, the subject of who was to play the part of Joan was discussed. Shaw, says Langner,

> had recently seen Alla Nazimova in the moving pictures (they were silent in those days) and thought she might be right for the part. Despite her accent I felt, however, that some quality of the character would be lost if it were not

played by a young girl. Eva Le Gallienne had been playing the part of Julie in *Liliom* with a great deal of spiritual quality, and I suggested her as the best possibility for the part.[4]

Shaw's choice was the strikingly beautiful Russian-born actress Mme Nasimoff, who had come to the United States in 1905 as the leading actress of Paul Orleneff's Russian Theatre, which he had established on the Lower East Side of New York. According to Henry Blum, "She created a sensation. Henry Miller brought her up-town. On November 13, 1906, with her name slightly altered, Alla Nazimova made her debut on the English-speaking stage in 'Hedda Gabler,' and soon she had joined the ranks of the truly great actresses of the American theatre."[5] Langner, in choosing Eva Le Gallienne, was opting for an English-born actress, also dark-haired and beautiful, who, although she was less well established in the American theatre than Nazimova, was certainly as promising.[6] The immediate difference was one of age. In 1923 Nazimova was forty-four (Shaw, remember, had the forty-year-old Sybil Thorndike in mind for the English première), while Eva Le Gallienne was only twenty-four. In retrospect, it seems that Langner was correct in rejecting the idea of Nazimova to play Joan. Apart from the drawbacks of her age and her accent (although this last seems to have been a point in her favour with Shaw, if the emphasis in Langner's statement quoted above is correct), her great talent clearly lay in portraying the troubled moods of Ibsen and Chekhov, rather than the intellectual clarity of Shaw. When, later, she did appear in a Shaw play (*The Simpleton of the Unexpected Isles* in 1935), it failed, and she immediately returned to Ibsen, playing Mrs. Alving in a revival of *Ghosts* with great success. Eva Le Gallienne would have done a better job, I believe: she possessed a more flexible playing range and style, was at home in Ibsen and Chekhov, but also made great success out of such widely divergent roles as Juliet and Peter Pan. Interestingly enough, both Shaw's choice for Joan and Langner's appeared together in a splendid revival of *The Cherry Orchard* in 1928.

Nevertheless, to neither of them fell the honour of portraying Shaw's saint for the first time, although some attempt does appear to have been made to engage Nazimova. After returning to New York, Langner wrote to Shaw explaining why his choice was not to play the part. He explained that Nazimova had had a "peculiar career"; he conceded her early artistry, but explained that since she had taken to acting in movies she had played mainly "exotic parts," and had not been in a successful play in New York for five years. Out of deference to Shaw's wishes, he went on, the Guild had discussed the part with Nazimova, but "she was tied up in a music hall engagement for two months and we were anxious to open with Joan during Christmas week."[7] Eva Le Gallienne is not mentioned by Langner, but informs me in a letter that she, too, was approached:

I was indeed offered the part of St. Joan by the Theatre Guild — but, with the temerity and arrogance of my 24 years, I refused the offer. I had been brought up in France and my ideas of "Jeanne d'Arc" were not those of Bernard Shaw. I remember saying to Mr. Langner that the play should have been called "St. Bernard Shaw" — since I felt it was Shaw speaking rather than Joan.[8]

No wonder, concludes Miss Le Gallienne, Langner did not mention her in his letter to Shaw!

In the absence of these candidates there seems to have been disagreement among the board of the Theatre Guild: "After a debate as to who should play the Saint, which lasted with undiminished violence for many days, the Board finally selected Winifred Lenihan for the part."[9] Certainly, like Eva Le Gallienne, Winifred Lenihan possessed the attributes of youth: "Miss Lenihan has youth, sincerity, a fine spiritual quality, a boyishness and real beauty, and she is one of the up-and-coming young women in our theatre."[10] Winifred Lenihan was twenty-five in 1923. A protegée of Winthrop Ames, her appearances in both *The Betrothal*, and *The Dover Road* had been successful, and she had only recently acted in a French play for the Guild entitled *The Failures* — appropriately enough, for it did not draw audiences, though it was, according to Langner, a fine play.[11] She turned out to be an excellent choice. As Langner stated later, "I have seen five productions of *Saint Joan* in three languages, and I have yet to see a performance to equal hers."[12] The actress herself was not satisfied with her own performance; notwithstanding the fact that the play was so successful that it had to be transferred to the larger Empire Theatre. She told Ada Patterson:

Do you want to know how I really felt on the night that *Saint Joan* moved to the Empire? I was conscious all through my performance of a serious handicap. I had rehearsed it while I was playing *Failures*. The role that I played in *Failures* was a very exacting one. There wasn't much energy left to give to the rehearsals of the Shaw play. I felt that I wasn't doing what I wanted to do with the part. But it could not be undone. A part settles into a mold, and you cannot break the mold. So that is the reason. I was unhappy on the night that was called a triumph. I was so unhappy that when a friend who is playing in another theatre, and a boy in the company and I, went to supper after the theatre at Childs' my tears dropped into the dishes I ordered.[13]

Part of her dissatisfaction lay with the part itself: "I don't like it [the part of Joan] myself. Shaw is irritating. Just as one begins to soar in a part he pulls a string, and brings her down with a bump."[14]

Whether Miss Lenihan's alternation of "soars" and "bumps" helped to impart an unevenness to the Garrick production it is difficult, at this date, to say. But all the critics of the first performance express a disunified response: a great admiration for certain scenes or moments, and an equally vehement dislike for others. The scene in which Joan "first uplifts the sword of France before the altar thrills mightily," wrote John Corbin of the *New York Times*. For him, as for many others, the "great triumph" of the play was the Trial Scene. Stark Young called the Loire Scene "the worst in the play." For John Farrar the direction in the Tent Scene was "deplorably bad." Gilbert Seldes found the Epilogue "dull in the theatre." Such comments suggest that the production itself was uneven. The tone of *Saint Joan* does change, but not by alternation so much as by progression. The play begins in light—almost comic—mood on a sunny day, and becomes progressively darker, both actually and dramatically, culminating in a night scene of symbolic intensity. This unity of conception seems to have been missed by critics of the world première, though the play seems to have improved in their minds in retrospect.[15]

According to Alice Griffin, the critical reception accorded to *Saint Joan* at its New York opening did not indicate that it would be a world masterpiece,[16] an opinion echoed by Irving McKee.[17] Apart from the obvious response, namely that most dramatic masterpieces from *The Way of the World* to *Ghosts* have drawn critical fire at their premières, the remarkable fact is that in spite of the uneven nature of the performance many New York critics *did* spot Shaw's play as a winner. Indeed, Griffin and McKee are somewhat selective in their critical examples, often overlooking some quite important critics, and occasionally omitting significant sentences in the critics they do cite. For example, McKee quotes John Corbin's *New York Times* review, in which he admittedly grumbles about the play's wordiness, but omits his comment that *Saint Joan* "is one of those Shaw plays, and they are among the best, that improve as one looks back at them." The main voices expressing disapproval seem to have been George Jean Nathan in the *American Mercury*, Gilbert Seldes in *Dial*, Percy Hammond in the *Tribune*, Kenneth MacGowan in *Theatre Arts Monthly*, and Stark Young in the *New Republic*. The rest of the critics, though some found fault with minor matters, praised the work. Ludwig Lewisohn in the *Nation* described the play as "obviously a first rate work by a first rate writer"; Stephen Rathbun of the *Sun and Globe* trod neutral ground but claimed that *Saint Joan* "should interest even theatregoers who will not give it their unqualified approval"; for John Farrar in the *Bookman* it was "one of the most satisfying plays of the season"; agreeing with him is Harold Kellock in the *Freeman* who states unequivocally, "If the dramatic season is to afford any more significant offering or any more substantial entertainment than 'Saint Joan,' the horizon as yet gives no sign of it." Heywood Broun of the *World* declares that it is "the finest play written in the English language in our day." And under the heading "Broadway is Inspired," Jack Crawford in the *Drama* writes,

Whatever else the theatrical season of 1924 may have in store for us, it has given us a play which may not again be equalled in this age. I refer to Bernard Shaw's *Saint Joan*. It is many months since I have permitted myself in these columns the luxury of enthusiasm. I feel certain now that it will be many months before I am enthusiastic again, because plays the like of this one occur at intervals of one hundred years apart, and once seen spoil the beholders for lesser stuff. This particular play is not only a triumph for the Theatre Guild, but also a milestone in the progress of the drama . . . There is only one play in New York.[18]

There was a great deal of praise, too, for Miss Lenihan's Joan.[19] To judge from the reviews, she seems to have captured with beauty and intelligence the simple, boyish, active aspects of Joan's character. Several critics (ironically in view of Langner's reasons for wanting Le Gallienne) felt that Lenihan lacked an "inner fire," a "flaming spirit," and a "spiritual vision," Seldes concluding that although her performance was "always interesting, always intelligent, it could not be moving." Others disagreed. R. C. Benchley in *Life* felt that she combined "the peasant crudities and spiritual exaltation of the Maid as we can imagine no other young actress of our stage doing." And at least one critic was moved to tears, stating: "More than once I found my eyes moist, and old theatre hounds do not easily weep. My thanks may not mean much to her, but I humbly offer them. And Mr. Shaw owes her his blessing too."[20]

Curiously enough, this was something Shaw never gave. Indeed, he remained non-committal about the American performance of his play, undoubtedly because of the Guild's panic over its length. They had written to Shaw in familiar vein, early in rehearsals, asking him to make some deletions, so that the suburban audience could catch their last trains home. His response was the now famous cable of 19 November 1923: THE OLD OLD STORY BEGIN AT EIGHT OR RUN LATER TRAINS AWAIT FINAL REVISION OF PLAY—SHAW. The Guild cabled Shaw to tell him that, since they were well into rehearsal, any postponement of the opening would cost them money and to ask him to hurry up with his revised version. This angered Shaw, who wrote waspishly to the effect that the revised version had been sent, and was shorter. Langner complains that the revisions omitted little from the unrevised proofs from which they had been rehearsing; a complaint that a comparison of drafts, such as we have undertaken, reveals to be justified. The dress rehearsal confirmed that the play was inconveniently long, another cable was sent, and after the opening night's reviews had underlined this criticism yet again, the Guild, still sensitive about *Back to Methuselah*, and irritated by the fact that some members of the audience were leaving before the final curtain, again sent Shaw desperate telegrams, which he ignored. They even persuaded Winifred Lenihan to cable in her own name to ask him to shorten the play; and to her Shaw

did reply: THE GUILD IS SENDING ME TELEGRAMS IN YOUR NAME, PAY NO ATTEN-
TION TO THEM—SHAW. Later, he was to rebuke Langner over this: "You ought to
be ashamed of yourselves for getting a young actress into trouble with an author
like that."[21] No doubt her telegram was a contributory reason for Shaw's coolness
about Winifred Lenihan's performance as the Maid, though the main one may
have been his loyalty to Sybil Thorndike. But this silence on the subject of Miss
Lenihan's performance at times grew very loud. He made no response to the
critical acclaim of her performance in the reviews sent to him by Langner; and
when Archibald Henderson, interviewing Shaw on 1 February 1924, claimed the
supremacy of the New York stage as regards acting, and even cited the Theatre
Guild's production of *Saint Joan* to prove it, Shaw handed no bouquet to the
young actress, but "passed on" (like Joan herself) to other matters.[22] Yet he must
have been impressed by what he read about her, for when Cardinal Hayes presented Miss Lenihan with a medal for her impersonation of the saint[23] Shaw did
not hesitate to make capital out of it;[24] and in 1928, when Winifred Lenihan was
picked to play Major Barbara in the Theatre Guild's revival of that play, Shaw
wrote to Theresa Helburn, co-director of the Theatre Guild, with what could be
interpreted as grudging confidence in her choice: "I do not suppose there is much
danger of Winifred Lenihan making Barbara a low-spirited person with large eyes,
looking like a picture on the cover of The Maiden's Prayer, though that is the
traditional stage view of a religious part."[25]

   Winifred Lenihan appeared as Saint Joan for 214 performances in New York,
but when it was decided to send the play on tour she declined to continue in the
part, to the detriment of her own career and of the production, in which Julia
Arthur was an inadequate substitute. Another illustration of Shaw's rather preju-
diced attitude towards the American production can be found in the matter of the
stage setting. In his original instructions to Langner Shaw said, "The scenes in
Joan can all be reduced to extreme simplicity. A single pillar of the Gordon Craig
type will make the cathedral. All the Loire needs is a horizon and a few of
Simonson's lanterns. The trial scene is as easy as the cathedral. The others present
no difficulty."[26] Accordingly, the Guild complied: "The keynote of the Guild's
production was its essential simplicity. Lee Simonson's scenery and costumes gave
it a stark, hard masculine quality which I have never seen in any other production, and the English presentation which Shaw raved about, and which I saw
later, struck me as very prettified and feminine indeed."[27] Langner's assessment of
the Guild's set is borne out by the display of photographs in *Theatre Magazine* for
March 1924. On one point, however, Langner is in error: the sets and costumes
were not Simonson's. Lee Simonson, in an amusing mock-melancholy letter to
Shaw, dated 30 December 1923, explained why he was unable to design the sets
for *Saint Joan*. However, he rejoiced with Shaw that his saint would not be
"stained with the slightest tinge of nicotine" (Simonson was a very heavy smoker,

and had been rebuked by Shaw for so being) because Raymond Sovey (the replacement) did not smoke. He describes Sovey's set: "His semi-permanent set is monumental in scale, decorative but not fantastic, true to the architectural spirit of the time, cleverly contrived so that the shifts are quick, but the different scenes seem really different, and not obviously rearranged out of the same elements."[28] Ironically, Langner's adverse comments on the set of the English production echo Shaw's remarks on Sovey's set when he saw the photographs of the American production:

> The altar and candles in the middle of the cathedral scene are feebly stagey and do not give the effect of a corner of a gigantic cathedral as my notion of one big pillar would. And it leads to that upstage effect, with a very feminine operatic-looking Joan in the centre which I wanted to avoid . . . but still it is all very pretty in the American way, and it might have been worse.[29]

He adds, "I am going to see Charles Rickett's plans and sketches for the London production this afternoon; and it will be interesting to see what he makes of them."[30] The comparison was, perhaps, invidious. Charles Ricketts' distinguished career as an artist and designer extended back into the 1890s, when he executed fine black and white designs for Oscar Wilde's "The Sphinx." Later he turned to wood engraving and designed three fonts of type for the Vale Press; through it he published fifty or sixty books, designing both the binding and the type. In addition, he was a fine oil painter, a member of the Royal Academy, and the set designer for some of the most notable stage productions of his day. He had designed for Shaw before at the Court Theatre; and now, with his friend Charles Shannon, was engaged to work on the scenery and costumes for *Saint Joan*; a fitting climax to a long career.

While Ricketts and Shannon worked on their designs they were living in the keep of Chilham Castle in Kent, and, according to Lillah McCarthy, "It was the kitchen of Chilham Castle that Ricketts used in designing the setting of the first scene in 'Saint Joan.'"[31] Lillah McCarthy was a friend of Ricketts and Shannon as well as of Shaw and, prior to its first English production, made great efforts to secure the part of Joan for herself:

> I begged him to let me play Joan, but it was not to be. I tried hard. I thought I had succeeded. To play the part of Joan I was ready to embark again on the treacherous seas of management. I got the option on two theatres: but Shaw was an older man now; though his brain was as good as ever. He must keep his strength for the work he had yet to do. Another actress—a justly famous one, Sybil Thorndike—was in the fulness of her powers, and was already in management. She could produce the play at once. Shaw would be saved all

the inevitable labour which, as he well knew, he must go through once we started on cast and company, scenery, dresses and production. I can sympathize with him and understand, but it made me very sad.[32]

That Shaw would "save himself labour" by entrusting the play and the part to Thorndike instead of McCarthy sounds like pure rationalization. As we have seen, his commitment to Sybil Thorndike was made before he began writing his play, and was made on artistic grounds.

Sybil Thorndike's commitment to Shaw now became a factor as she could *not* produce the play "at once." In February 1924, she was still appearing as Eleanor Shale in *The Lie*, by Henry Arthur Jones, which was showing no signs of a diminishing box office. Finally, "Sybil and Lewis, to say nothing of Mr. Shaw, got restive, and 'The Lie' was withdrawn when playing to good money, and 'Saint Joan' was put up."[33] Later, on 30 May 1925, the Cassons revived *The Lie* successfully at Wyndham's Theatre; but its withdrawal from the New Theatre on 22 March, 1924, while playing to packed houses for 187 performances, increased its author's resentment towards Shaw.[34]

On 24 February 1924, while *Saint Joan* was still playing to capacity crowds in New York, Shaw wrote to Molly Tompkins: "I start rehearsing Saint Joan tomorrow, Heaven help me!"[35] According to Shaw, his rehearsal technique was invariable. He explained his procedure at rehearsal to Henderson in 1926:

I have a very precise system, whereas other producers, I am told, vary between a haphazard and—for the unfortunate actors—contemptuously inconsiderate succession of interruptions and wrangles which makes it astonishing that the play is produced at all, and a rigid dictation by the producer in which the actors are reduced to puppets, and are expected to reproduce even the exact tones of the producer's voice, which they sometimes revenge themselves by doing only too faithfully; so that the whole company gives ridiculous imitations of the producer instead of acting. Neither in this matter nor in any other have I ever changed my procedure.[36]

That procedure is set out clearly in Shaw's article, "Rules for Directors," in which he speaks of the choosing of the cast according to age, personality, and voice.[37] That Shaw himself supervised some of the casting is evident from the testimony of Jack Hawkins, who played Dunois' page.

Jack Hawkins, at thirteen, had appeared only once before professionally, tutored by the Contis in *Where the Rainbow Ends*. Now, Italia Conti, presumably contacted by the Cassons for likely child talent, summoned him to an audition at the New Theatre; and meeting him and his mother at the stage door explained that he was to audition for the part of a pageboy in a new play by Bernard Shaw. Hawkins continues:

I barely had time to take in all this, or even think whether this was what I wanted before we were summoned to a dressing room where Sybil Thorndike and her husband, Lewis Casson, were waiting. I was aware of another person in the room, apparently perched on the mantelpiece, dressed in very hairy tweeds, and with a mass of red hair on his face and head. Lewis Casson handed me a few pages of typescript and told me to read the part of Dunois' page with him. I had hardly got to the end of the first line, when George Bernard Shaw, for that was who he was, clambered down from his precarious seat, and snatched the papers from me with a ferocious cry of "No, boy! Like THIS," and in a ridiculous falsetto read: "Look, look! There she goes." I thought he was quite mad, but nevertheless tried to mimic him.[38]

In "Rules for Directors," Shaw also speaks of his practice of reading the play aloud to the company. Of his remarkable solo performance before Sybil Thorndike and her company much has been written.[39] For Thorndike, who allegedly heard him read the play three times, Shaw had some additional advice: "When I saw G.B.S., he asked had I read the histories about Joan. 'Every single one,' I said. 'Then forget them,' he said. 'I'll tell you what to think.' And I, feeling like a Russian Communist, was content to be told what to think."[40] Interesting in view of Shaw's opposition to the concept of dictator-director is his belief, expressed in 1949, that the director should come to the first rehearsals, "with the stage business thoroughly studied, and every entry, movement, rising and sitting, disposal of hat and umbrella, etc.,...settled ready for instant dictation."[41] A week, Shaw insisted, should be spent on stage movements, book in hand, with the director on the stage; two weeks while the play is being memorized and performed by the actors, with the director offstage taking notes; and a week for the dress rehearsals, with the director on stage again, "directing and interrupting ad lib."[42] One may assume this to have been the manner in which *Saint Joan* was rehearsed, since the play was a month in rehearsal, and we have it on Blanche Patch's authority that "on his own rehearsal copies of the plays he had worked out the precise mechanics of each. Saint Joan must stand just here; Dunois there; the Dauphin over yonder. Each must speak as directed, each when silent must be silent in a natural way."[43]

An example of Shaw's meticulous attention to detail is implied in a letter to Shaw from Stogumber Vicarage, Somerset, dated 14 March 1924, obviously written in response to a request from Shaw, asserting that the name Stogumber "is pronounced Sto-gumber—the accent is on the middle syllable.... The word which looks and sounds so strange, is a corruption of Stoke-de-Gomer."[44] However, a letter from Shaw to Molly Tompkins suggests that his control over the cast in this production was less than one would assume from the foregoing: "I did not drill anybody in St. Joan. I took more than a thousand notes in my big red notebook, all about trifles, and did the drudgery for them; but they were all as free as they wanted to be."[45] Indeed, although Shaw no doubt felt fully responsible for the production and, according to Russell Thorndike (who describes him as the "producer"), "knew every intonation he wanted,"[46] Raymond Massey, who played both La Hire and D'Estivet, indicates that directing honours seem to have been shared between Shaw and Lewis Casson: "We all assumed that Lewis Casson was the director. But this function was still a novelty in England in 1924, and in any case, Shaw would impose his wishes on all concerned regardless of custom."[47] Nor, it seems, was there total agreement between the two halves of the directing team:

> The most significant feature of the London production of Shaw's play was the disagreement between Shaw and Lewis Casson in the matter of pace. Shaw's one concern was the protection of his precious lines. He would not cut out a word and if he had had his own way the play would have lasted four hours. Lewis had the almost impossible task of getting the final curtain down in time for the suburban customers to catch suitable trains and also to keep them awake in face of the leisurely amble which the author demanded from the players.... Shaw attended all morning rehearsals about 3 hours long, and would sprinkle quotes on performance like confetti. Lewis would repair the damage in the afternoon when G.B.S. was not there taking at least 5 minutes playing time out of each act. Shaw finally about dress rehearsals time gave up, and that matchless company and Lewis himself as de Stogumber triumphed over the frustration and confusion.[48]

Lewis Casson himself, speaking of Shaw's part in the production, found fault with his handling of the Epilogue:

> There is assuredly an intensely comic idea in the canonisation of a Saint by the Church that had burned her. But at the first production he so over-emphasized this with overplaying and funny business, that although Ernest Thesiger and I induced him to modify this considerably at rehearsal, it still shocked the audience far more than was necessary and marred the essential beauty of the play's design.[49]

Ernest Thesiger played the Dauphin, and others in the cast included Eugene Leahy as Cauchon, Robert Horton as Dunois, E. Lyall Swete as Warwick, Lawrence Anderson as Ladvenu, and O. B. Clarence as the Inquisitor.

The dress rehearsals were not without incident. Jack Hawkins pays tribute to the stage manager, Thomas Warren, in the following anecdote, concerning the end of Scene III:

I was perched on a hillock guarding Dunois' great shield and lance. At the end of the scene, when Dunois and Joan were leaving the stage, I had to tug the lance from the ground, pick up the shield, and jump down to the rostrum, and from there down three steps to stage level, shouting: "The Maid, the Maid! God and the Maid! Hurray-ay-ay!"

Then, according to the stage directions, I was to "caper out after them, mad with excitement." I followed these directions faultlessly, but by the time I hit the stage level I had lost control of the heavy lance. The point swung forward and plunged through the extremely beautiful stage drop which was then coming down. There was a horrified silence, and I was close to tears when I saw the damage I had done. Tommy Warren stalked across the stage and without a word carefully extracted the lance from the rent in the drop. Then he turned to me. I expected a frightful blasting, possibly even dismissal, but he simply said: "Don't worry, boy. It's not your fault. We should have tested this out long before now."[50]

Russell Thorndike reports another

amusing incident at dress rehearsal, which thoroughly pleased Sybil. Charles Ricketts had done all the wonderful designs and dresses for the play when Mr. Shaw came on to the stage and said: "Scenery and clothes have ruined my play. Why can't you play it in plain clothes as at rehearsal? Sybil is much more like Joan in her ordinary jumper and skirt than when dressed up like this, with her face all painted." Sybil jumped for joy. She hates scenery, hates costumes, and always says she can act better with a towel round her head and her face ordinary.[51]

One may take leave to doubt whether her joy was shared by Charles Ricketts; and indeed, according to Lillah McCarthy,

the association between [Shaw and Ricketts] seemed to end sadly for, while Ricketts reached the summit of his career in the designing of the scenes and costumes for "St. Joan," he also suffered disappointment in his admiration for Shaw. "He was a sympathetic producer in the old days," he wrote to me. "His little lectures in the wings and exaggerated renderings of what he wanted were delightful. Today, he only thinks of his points and, I believe, dislikes good acting and productions.[52]

The comments of Raymond Massey and Charles Ricketts do seem to prove that in his later years Shaw really did concentrate overmuch on the spoken word to the exclusion of presentation; and certainly some of the exasperated anger of

Gordon Craig can be traced to this source.[53] It is interesting, therefore, to note that in an open letter to Craig in April 1926, defending himself primarily against the charge of "thrusting aside too many a real English artist playwright," Shaw refers in kindly terms to the two most offended parties in the *Saint Joan* production, saying of the first, "Now the truth is that I could not get my last play into the theatre until Henry Arthur Jones gracefully made way for me by suspending the performance of a play of his which was still unexhausted after a long run."[54] As we have seen, it was with a very bad grace that Henry Arthur Jones made way for him, a bad grace underlined by Shaw's admission later in his article that Jones' misanthropy "has taken a most unfortunate turn for me."[55] In the same article Shaw pays a handsome compliment to Ricketts, which may have been intended to placate that gentleman, and may also have been in part due to the reviews of the London production, which were unanimously enthusiastic about its set designs and costumes: "I am actually asked what would St. Joan have been without Ricketts: and I am obliged to confess that it would have been a mere sketch in black and white."[56]

Saint Joan opened at the New Theatre on Wednesday, 26 March 1924. The public showed great interest in the production. Queues for tickets formed at 5:00 A.M. on the morning of the opening night, and the *Daily Mirror* reported that "more than two thousand people, including several duchesses" had been turned away from the box office of the New Theatre.[57] In the words of Russell Thorndike, "If ever there was an electric first night, Joan's was."[58] Supplying not a little of the voltage was A. B. Walkley, influential critic of *The Times*, who on the day of the premiere published an article which began with the words, "We are to have tonight a play about Joan of Arc, and it is to be hoped it will not be disfigured by those blithe anachronisms and incongruities of treatment with which Mr. Bernard Shaw in his quasi-historical plays occasionally delights to criticize the present through the past."[59] The bulk of the article concerned Anatole France's book on Joan, which Walkley had been reading; but ended with the devout hope that Shaw would do the Maid justice. Walkley, together with his critical brethren, took his seat that night amid distinguished company, which included many friends and acquaintances of Shaw. Archibald Henderson gives this account:

> Thanks to G.B.S., I was seated in the third row of the stalls, immediately behind three friends, Henry Arthur Jones, William Archer, and Granville Barker on the opening night of the play at the New Theatre. At the intermission I escorted the gifted cartoonist Bohun Lynch, who had never seen Shaw, up to the box where we chatted with G.B.S., Charlotte, and Lena Ashwell [later Lady Simson]. Before the curtain fell, I asked my three friends if they would join me in a call for the author, but my dignified friends declined. As the curtain fell, I led off with the Confederate "rebel

yell," which I had learned from my father and uncle who fought under Lee in the Civil War; and was followed by more decorous applause and calls for "Author! Author!" Walkley left before the manager appeared before the curtain and announced regretfully that the author was not in the house.[60]

According to Walkley's review in *The Times*, "Miss Thorndike said they were looking for him, but whether they found him or not we could not wait to see. The cast, meanwhile, took a dozen curtain calls."[61] Walkley's haste to be off, however, was not because of his desire to make amends for his earlier lack of faith. His review immediately pounced upon the Epilogue as an example of what he had most feared, the "Shavianization of the story." Other critics agreed; and Shaw was correct when he wrote to Langner identifying the length and the Epilogue of the play as being the parts singled out for adverse comment. He was also substantially right when he claimed: "The play has repeated its American success here: it is going like mad; and everyone, to my disgust, assures me that it is the best play I have ever written."[62] But his next sentence is open to question: "Sybil Thorndike's acting and Charles Ricketts' stage pictures have carried everything before them."[63] About Ricketts' designs and costumes there is no question. They were singled out time and again for separate praise. On the subject of Thorndike's acting, however, the critics were not unanimous; and although most praised her in the part, nearly all had reservations. Walkley, who wrote in *The Times*, that she performed beautifully, also thought her "rusticity of speech a superfluity." The critic of the *Daily Telegraph*, for whom no other actress could have better "hit off the Maid's simplicity without losing her strength," admitted, "She does not grip the imagination entirely in the first two scenes." Desmond MacCarthy in the *New Statesman*, while praising Thorndike for emphasizing the "insistive, energetic, almost pert traits of the Maid as Mr. Shaw conceives her," yet complained that "the sweetness and simplicity of the Maid's replies and demeanour in the trial scene she does not bring out. Her distress, her alertness, her courage, she does drive home, but whether the fault lies in the part itself or in the interpretation 'the angelic side' of the Maid is obscured."[64] No critic was quite so negative about Sybil Thorndike's performance as was that of the *Bookman*, who believed that "Miss Thorndike fails completely. She acted without imaginative force, without passion, without any depth. Her accent—presumably of Mr. Shaw's own choosing—hovered between Oldshire and a Dublin brogue. She was restless and hopelessly 'girlish.' The truth is Miss Thorndike was badly miscast."[65]

In addition to the public reviews, the friends and acquaintances of Bernard Shaw also expressed mixed feelings about the production. Blanche Patch, for example, who had been impressed when typing the scene after the burning of Joan where de Stogumber rushes in and cries that he will be damned, was disappointed in it at the first performance.[66] Henderson, lunching with the Shaws on the afternoon following the first night, found fault with "the clever, but stagey overplaying of Ernest Thesiger as the Dauphin," the "spotless armor, as if just arrived from Wardour Street," and the Epilogue, which he frankly deplored as a "Shavian gloss upon the play."[67] And Shaw's correspondence discloses a hitherto unpublished criticism of Sybil Thorndike's performance as Joan, from the painter Laurence Alma Tadema; a letter which grumbles about the "Alice-in-Wonderland Court," and complains that Shaw cannot distinguish between wit and buffoonery, and then goes on to blame the faults of the production on Sybil Thorndike! She is described as a "coarse actress": "She did only one thing well — the *terror* of her judgement scene. But she has no power of portraying innocence or the eyes of youth or faith. Her first impression was disastrous: instead of smelling of the open air, of grass or sheep, of spun lambs' wool, she smelt of a tea-shop."[68]

Time is a great maker of legends; and the legend of Sybil Thorndike's Joan will remain in theatrical history in spite of the caution of the critic. Shaw himself, who once described his own reputation as founded upon a basis of dogmatic reiteration, certainly helped. Replying to Leslie Rees' questionnaire[69] in 1934, Shaw, asked if people missed the point of his play, said, "The point was certainly not missed in England. Miss Thorndike, who established the English tradition of the part, hit it exactly."[70] But in spite of the evident power she brought to the part there seems to be sufficient consistency in the criticisms of her performance to make it difficult to agree entirely with J. C. Trewin's assessment: "Joan was one of the overwhelming performances of the half century.... Joan, as Sybil Thorndike played her, grew to a pillar of faith and fire. She had a timeless quality. No one has forgotten the radiance of her belief."[71] During the eight years from 1924 to 1932, Thorndike played the Maid in no less than seven separate productions, taking the play to France, South Africa, and Australia. In 1941 she returned to the role in a charity matinee at the Palace. And although on 25 January 1945, her daughter Ann Casson opened as Joan, in a production that still included two of the original 1924 cast, Lewis Casson and Eugene Leahy, Sybil herself was not yet ready to relinquish the role. She performed parts of it in her extensive poetry recital tour of Australia, New Zealand, Tasmania, India, Hong Kong, and Malaya in the summer of 1954, and played the part in its entirety for the last time on BBC radio in 1967 at the age of eighty-five!

In the very month (March 1924) that the London critics were discussing *Saint Joan*, it also became the talk of Paris. M. Thomas, New York correspondent to *Comoedia* mounted a powerful attack on the play, implying that Shaw had insulted the French national heroine. His article led to a spirited defence of Shaw by Augustin Hamon (Shaw's official translator into French); and this led to a further onslaught from Thomas and from Gabriel Boissy. Finally, Shaw himself joined in, contributing an article to *Comoedia*, which later appeared in English in the *New York Times*. In it Shaw was good-humoured, but severe. Paris is described as "not only as uncivilized as New York or London but ... suffering from a special kind of Eighteenth Century provincialism." He doubts whether the French stage will accord him the politeness granted him by other European stages. Nothing, he avers, can be done:

> I have educated London. I have educated New York, Berlin and Vienna: Moscow and Stockholm are at my feet, but I am too old to educate Paris; it is too far behind and I am too far ahead. Besides this, my method of education is to teach people how to laugh at themselves, and the pride of Paris is so prodigious that it has beaten all its professors from Moliere to Anatole France and might even beat me.[72]

This was hardly the kind of talk likely to predispose the French playgoer to the teaching of Bernard Shaw, or to cheer the heart of anyone brave enough to produce his latest work in Paris!

The task of so doing fell the following year to perhaps the most remarkable producer and actress in Europe at that time, the famous Pitoëffs. Although it was only six years since their brilliant production of Lenormand's *Les Ratés* had led to their "discovery" by the Paris critics, they had been in the vanguard of theatre for over a decade. Georges Pitoëff, born in Georgia, Russia, and son of a theatrical director, had been involved in theatre all his life, directing plays in Russia and Switzerland, where, in 1914, he met his wife-to-be, Ludmilla, also from Tiflis, Georgia. The pair ran a most successful acting company at the Plain-Palais, Geneva, until 1919, when they came to Paris. Subsequently they had performed Ibsen, Tolstoy, Pirandello, Chekhov, Cocteau, and many others. In 1925 they planned the French première of *Saint Joan*.

Not surprisingly, in view of the above, they did so with some misgiving, as Aniouta Pitoëff reveals in his book *Ludmilla ma mère*:

> A fairly well-spaced correspondence had always managed to answer the Pitoëffs' desire to retain Shaw's respect and encouragement. At the time of *Saint Joan* the exchange of letters multiplied. Each week, the Pitoëffs reported to us the celebrated Irish author's advice and recommendations lavished on them in a pleasant, often very comical manner. Everyone would be amused by this. But the closer they got to the dress rehearsal, the more difficult it became for the Pitoëffs to conceal their anxiety. What reception would be given this masterpiece? Would the hostility of one segment of the press and of the Parisian public towards G. B. Shaw and his plays, scarcely one of which had succeeded in France, find a new excuse to break out? The spirit of the play, its flavour, its truth, the new range of its resonances deli-

berately chased away the ancient obscure or partisan mystiques of the history of the Maid of Orleans. For after all, he was trying to present to the French public a marvellous chronicle of their national heroine, canonized only in 1920—a chronicle in the form of a play written by an Irishman and presented and played by two Russians. Moreover, Shaw's thought was clear in it. His explanation of Joan's case was extreme. Through the idea of homeland, which was incarnate in her, he had made the Maid into a *nationalist*, forgetting the entire feudal hierarchy, and a *Protestant* through her free inquiry, which enabled her to communicate directly with God. However, "Rome did not believe it had canonized a Protestant!"

"How are they going to take this play?" sighed Ludmilla.

Would not the legitimate susceptibilities of national purists and Catholics run the risk of exploding? Will this be a *succès d'estime*, a triumph or a catastrophe? The sums of money invested in this affair were enormous.[73]

In addition to the amount of money, Aniouta Pitoëff's book testifies to the enormous amount of energy invested in the production; but it seems evident that the play's monumental success was due to a number of factors.

First, as Daniel C. Gerould points out, since the end of World War I the poetic drama in France had been dying and the French critics were favourably disposed towards a non-poetic, realistic treatment of Joan of Arc, having just witnessed the failure of François Porche's romantically pious presentation of the Maid in *La Vierge au grand coeur* at the Théâtre de la Renaissance, in January 1925.[74] Second, the Pitoëff production of *Sainte Jeanne* was the first Shaw play the Parisian public had experienced in a translation revised by a man of the theatre. The Pitoëffs, delighted with Shaw's original script (which he had sent them personally) were appalled by the translation they received from Augustin and Henriette Hamon, Shaw's official translators. The Hamons had been acting in that capacity for Shaw since 1907; but his choice of this husband and wife team can only be described as capricious.[75] Shaw himself, whose own French was poor, seems to have disagreed with them over parts of *Sainte Jeanne*[76] but not as violently as the Pitoëffs, who invited the playwright H.-R. Lenormand, to help them revise the Hamon text. Later, when this fact leaked out, via André Antoine's review of the play, it drew complaints from Hamon, and jeers from Shaw.[77] Aniouta Pitoëff complains that too much has been made of the text alterations,[78] but Lenormand tells in his book how he and Ludmilla spent some weeks revising the script.[79] Another effort of Georges Pitoëff to assure a favourable reception for *Sainte Jeanne* was apparently habitual with him. He invited all his friends and all the influential critics to the dress rehearsal, and then planned their seating in the auditorium, taking great care to place certain critics next to certain friends so that they would overhear only favourable comments and, separated from their critical brethren, be unable to conspire against the piece! This apparently worked well in the case of *Sainte Jeanne*. A final reason for the critical acclaim with which the play was received was quite simply Ludmilla Pitoëff.

This remarkable actress, from the beginning, in Georges Pitoëff's conception, dominated the entire play: "Before working out his theatrical production, Pitoëff marked a tiny point on a white page saying: 'This is Ludmilla.' Then, around this symbolic point the sketches of the scenery and of the triptych imposed themselves quite naturally."[80] Unfortunately for Shaw's conception of Joan, Ludmilla's personality was best able to express the kind of angelic frailty which he had striven so assiduously to efface from the portrait:

> Always pathetically human, even when she attained the summit of sublimity, Ludmilla, in her role of a delicate virgin so moving, but always valiant, impudent and self-willed, was transfigured by an inner radiance which exalted her. What an accent of truth in her replies! And what simple gravity in her youthful gestures! After the great trial scene she had become no more than a small broken body which the stage manager in the wings would take in his arms.[81]

Shaw was unaware of this, and Gerould's statement that "Shaw himself had an opportunity to see the Pitoëffs' production of *Saint Joan* when the French company came to London before the opening in Paris," is a half-truth; for he certainly had not seen Ludmilla in the part by December 1925, when he wrote to Molly Tompkins:

> I really cannot stand your not going to the Théatre des Arts and telling me whether la Pitoëff (to whom I have just posted a most lovilly portrait of myself in a copy of the Ricketts *edition de luxe* of St. Joan) is really so exquisite all over as she seems to be from her pictures, and from the ravings of all who have seen her in the part . . . Go at once I order you.[82]

It was Henri Bernstein, boulevard playwright, who stated outright that the success of *Sainte Jeanne* in Paris was achieved in spite of Shaw, since Ludmilla's acting contradicted every line of the text. Shaw, according to Frank Harris, "made fun of Bernstein to his heart's content; but later on, when he had seen Ludmilla's performance, he confessed that Bernstein was the one critic who had said exactly the right thing."[83] Shaw saw Ludmilla play the part in 1930; his unfavourable reaction was recorded by Leslie Rees: "Ludmilla Pitoëff . . . revived the snivelling womanly heroine of the old sentimental melodramas with appalling intensity. But the effect she made in Paris was not repeated in London, and will never, I hope, overcome that made by Miss Thorndike in London."[84] In view of Shaw's reaction to Ludmilla's performance, perhaps it is as well that we do not possess his comments on all the other eager aspirants who lined up to play his heroine in the first years of her theatrical life.

Siegfried Trebitsch, Shaw's German translator, had journeyed to London to meet Shaw and hear the new play in November 1923. He was understandably nervous. As a German he needed, in addition to a visa, a certificate from a British subject stating that Trebitsch's presence in England was either necessary or profitable to him: "Shaw had written me a whimsical letter for this purpose which I was to show at the frontier. It served its purpose and put the stern passport-inspectors in the highest good-humour."[85]

Shaw met him at Victoria Station and drove him through growing darkness to Ayot St. Lawrence, where they were greeted by Charlotte. They discussed the terrible war years that had separated them, the recent success in Birmingham of *Back to Methuselah*, and then Shaw read him *Saint Joan*. "Shaw reads with tremendous intensity. Every word is alive, the least of his scenes showing its necessity in the clearest light. At once I understood why he stands out more stubbornly against cuts than most other authors... The organic unity of each sentence, the literary quality of Shaw's diction, are obvious."[86] Trebitsch left "haunted" by the memory of the play's human and literary beauty. The German first production directed by Max Reinhardt at the Deutsches Theater, Berlin, in 1924 was a success, and a decade later Shaw was to have high praise for Elisabeth Bergner, who made "the world fall in love with a Catholic saint... when she created the part of Joan in Protestant Berlin when my play was new."[87]

But on 9 August 1925, Shaw wrote to Molly Tompkins about the forthcoming Italian first night: "Gramatica [*sic*] is going to play Santa Giovanna. Oh, these Joans! there is no end of them. It was from the Berlin one that I caught influenza.[88]

Each successive interpretation of Shaw's play seemed to move it farther from his original conception, but his complaints grew feebler, and finally stopped altogether. Perhaps his own recent experience as a translator gave him pause: his version of *Frau Gitta's Sühne* by Siegfried Trebitsch, called *Jitta's Atonement*, was performed for the first time in England at the Grand Theatre, Fulham, London, on 3 February 1925, the author complaining good-humouredly, "You have made my last act almost a comedy,"[89] but, as Shaw points out, he soon found that a literal translation would fail completely "to convey the play to an Anglo-American audience. It was necessary to translate the audience as well as the play."[90]

From Shaw's standpoint 1925 was not a good year for translations of his play. As early as June 1924 he had received a letter requesting permission for *Saint Joan* to be put on by the Kamerney Theatre of Moscow.[91] Permission was given, and the play performed. The result is best described by Robert Benchley, who saw their version in Vienna, whence he wrote on 19 July 1925:

We haven't much money left, but we would gladly give fifteen or twenty dollars of it (a little over a million kronen in vanilla money) to watch George Bernard Shaw's face at a performance of his "St. Joan" such as is being given here by the Russians of Tairoff's *Kammertheater*. If he is the man that he ought to be, he would laugh his head off.

For these Russian boys have taken his sacred script, which the New York Theatre Guild nearly bled itself to death over, and have put it on with boards and gunny-sack and made a circus of it. The characters, with the exception of Joan, are clowns. The settings are thrown together out of ill-fitting laths. The Dauphin, in actual clown make-up, with a little hat on the side of his head and a long feather trailing to one side, sits on an arrangement of boards like the bleachers at the Polo Grounds, clad in skin tights with a tiny dab of imperial ermine on the shoulders, and giggles pleasantly while huge bulbous-nosed churchmen discuss the state of the realm. The soldiers wear flannel uniforms, with nominal tin fittings to suggest armor, and tomato-can helmets. The Maid alone is immune from the devastating parody.

All this, of course, sharpens the satire to the point of burlesque and makes it a hundred times more malign. If Shaw really means to kid his country-men, if the centuries and centuries of repetition of the same old historic formulas, the pomp and ceremony and the majestic clash of arms, are to him the bunk that they seem to be, then he ought to adopt these Russians as his sons. If he is sore at what they have done, he doesn't understand his Shaw, that's all.[92]

Shaw *was* "sore" at what they had done. Harry Toogood quotes *Izvestia* as saying that Shaw did not like very much the way his "Joan" was interpreted by Tairoff.[93] Perhaps the resentment was not one-sided. There came a rumour in January 1925 that because of a letter Shaw had written to the Moscow *Izvestia* criticizing Zinovieff and other Russian leaders, the authorities planned to stop the run of *Saint Joan* at the Kamerney Theatre. However, the following month Alexander Tairoff, the director, denied that any attempt had been made to prohibit the play. At the same time he added a revealing remark which suggests that Shaw's irrita-tion with the Russian production was justified: "There was practically nothing eliminated from the original text except a few phrases which might convey the impression of a miraculous nature in certain events."[94]

Miraculous or not, there was no stopping the travels of his theatrical saint; and it would seem that the comment in the *Living Age* on 8 May 1926 is no more than the truth: "Probably no play of the last decade has had a vogue of anything like the scope and liveliness that Mr. Shaw's *Saint Joan* has enjoyed from the beginning."[95] After referring to revivals of Shaw's play underway in London, Berlin, and Paris, the author goes on to describe the most recent "first nights," those in Madrid and Belgrade. The play with Margarita Xirgu as the Maid was apparently received with favour by the Spanish audiences, in spite of the fears of those who felt its acceptance by the most Catholic capital in Europe was doubtful; and it was a success, too, when performed by the Zagreb National Theatre in Yugoslavia (it was the fifth of Shaw's plays to be given in Serbian), where "the emphasis on national consciousness could not fail to please a people that is still in the stage of idealistic nationalism in which France and England were in the time of Joan."[96] After Shaw was shown a photograph of Vika Podgorska, who played the title role in Belgrade, he is alleged to have remarked, "beautiful but not a bit like Saint Joan," though according to the critic of the *Graphic*, had he seen the performance he would have forgiven her for looking too pretty, and admitted that her conception of it was masterly.[97] Finally, from even further afield comes the report of Paul Scheffer, a German correspondent of the *Berliner Tageblatt*, who in 1926 visited the native theatre in Tokyo:

> I saw there Bernard Shaw's *Saint Joan* presented in a way that would have given the creeps to its irrepressible author. It was a hopeless hodgepodge of misconceptions regarding Europe. The historical costumes were caricatures — red wigs for blonde hair — and the actors had no conception of how to behave on the stage. When they were not speaking their hands hung down, with the little finger precisely at the trouser seam, like those of soldiers on parade. All that I learned from the play was that Japan is half the circumference of the globe from France. Not a single member of the troupe had ever been in Europe. The actors had learned what they knew of our continent out of books and newspapers, and assumed offhand that whatever amuses Westerners is typical of their civilization.[98]

Whatever the merits of the Japanese version (and one feels that Scheffer has not taken into account the need to "translate" the audience) the performance stands as proof of the extent to which in three short years *Saint Joan* had captured world attention.

7

Lasting Impressions

Scholarly and critical assessments were forthcoming as soon as *Saint Joan* was published in 1924. In *The Times Literary Supplement* Constable had announced as early as January of that year the future publication of *St. Joan: A Play* (Price 6/-); on 3 April they were still proclaiming its imminent arrival,[1] while on 22 May it was still "in preparation." Not until 26 June did a full-scale half-column advertisement appear in *TLS* with the words "Published yesterday" on it; at which time it had to compete with Leon Denis's *The Mystery of Joan of Arc* (translated by Conan Doyle), which was reviewed by *TLS* on that very day. By October an *édition de luxe* illustrated by Charles Ricketts and limited to 750 copies had appeared, priced at five guineas.

The delay in publication was no doubt occasioned by Shaw's careful work on the Preface, for which he consulted more works of reference.[2] Although in its original form the Preface was divided into the sections which are still found in the printed version, it did not contain section headings, Shaw merely signalling each new section with the sign like a large capital letter "I" that he had used to separate speakers in the play itself. One or two complete sections were inserted after the main outline of the Preface was finished, including "The Law of Change Is the Law of God," and "To the Critics, Lest They Should Feel Ignored"; but the process of correction seems to have been continuous, the alterations varying from the addition or deletion of single words to the excision of whole sentences and, in a couple of cases, fairly long paragraphs. It is regrettable that exigency of space makes it impossible to analyse all of Shaw's corrections in the Preface; for to read it is to appreciate keenly the meticulous way in which he builds up his argument, balancing word with word, phrase with phrase, yet always achieving a final effect of smooth-flowing spontaneity. It will perhaps be of greatest interest to look at one or two of the longer pieces that he later omitted.

For example, Shaw's awareness of Joan's bourgeois background, to which de Baudricourt makes reference in Scene I, is elaborated upon in the Preface, and then subsequently removed, originally appearing in the section now entitled "Joan's Social Position":

As a child Joan could please herself at times with being the young lady of the castle. Her mother had made a pilgrimage to Rome, and they called the [sic] Roman on that account. These details, establishing the fact that Joan's father was a proprietor, an organizer, and a man of business, suitably married to a woman with wider views and knowledge of life than those of a simple businesswoman, need [to] be insisted on to check the inveterate tendency of popular romance to insist that every hero or heroine must be either a prince or a beggar.[3]

Such a cut, made no doubt for considerations of length and relevancy, seems to me different from others which appear to have been made to reduce possible adverse reaction when the play was printed. In the section called "Catholicism Not Yet Catholic Enough," the second sentence originally ran like this: "If the Catholic Church, having canonized her, is to become catholic in fact as well as in name, it must, I think, frankly cease to nurture Joan's private revelations as supernatural revelations and admit that no official organization of mortal men, [etc.]"[4] This rebuke is grandly elaborated upon at the end of the first paragraph in that section, thus:

What is wrong with the Church is that the entrance to it is blocked up by superstitious rubbish. It is not the dogmas that matter: there is not a Protestant alive who does [not] cherish all the Catholic dogmas in one form or another in addition to a private collection which would expose a cardinal to the risk of excommunication. It is inessential trifles like insisting that the Blessed Virgin prefers smoky wax candles to electric light, and that a dead body that has disappeared by decomposition can undergo the miracle of resurrection whereas one that has disappeared in a civilized manner through cremation is lost for ever, that put people off the churches much more than the clogging of the essential doctrines with a demand for belief in legends which, though as bizarre as records of fact as any of the extravagances in Voltaire's La Pucelle, are yet not more incredible than much of the contents of our newspapers. It is not through losing contact with heavenly things that the churches grow emptier and emptier, and have to be desecrated and sold while theatres command monstrously inflated rents, but by losing contact with common sense. Tradition is a standby for people who are so behind-hand that they can give no better reason for their acts of faith than that they are doing what was done last time; but the law of evolution is a law of change; the law of God in any sense of the word which can now command responsible faith is the law of evolution; consequently the law of God is the law of change, and whenever any Church sets itself against change as such, it is setting itself against the law of God.[5]

The above is entirely removed, and replaced by a paragraph about a letter from a Catholic priest who, seeing in Shaw's play the conflict of "Regal, sacerdotal and Prophetical powers" ventured to suggest that it was not their conflict, but their "fruitful interaction" that would bring "peace and the Reign of the Saints." Father Leonard was Shaw's correspondent; and no doubt his call for a truce led to the excision of the above rebuke to the Catholic Church.

A final passage removed from the original Preface when it came to be printed reveals that Shaw was still upset by the American reception of his play. It was not so much the "yawning indifference" of the critics which angered Shaw as the extremism evident in those who professed like or dislike for the play. As we have seen, Winifred Lenihan was presented with a medal by a cardinal for performing the part of Joan; and on 30 November 1923 the "Joan of Arc Statue Committee" of the city of New York wrote to Shaw expressing their great interest in his play and asking for a copy. The letter goes on: "May I enquire what inspired you to write the play of this notable character?"[6] On the top of the letter, in Shaw's neat handwriting are the words, "Say that Saint Joan is not yet published, and that I hope to send him a copy when one is available. I presume it was Joan herself who inspired me to write it."[7] And one assumes that it was the presentation of medals, and organizations like the "Joan of Arc Statue Committee" which inspired Shaw to write in the original version of the Preface:

> I have no hope, however, that my play will enlighten anyone who is not enlightened already. I see by the notices of its first performance [in New York] that some of its critics have seen it as they have read the Bible: that is, in what is called the proper spirit, meaning the extremely improper spirit of the blind and deaf resolution to find there what you expect to find, without regard to the plainest statements to the contrary, or the most glaring omissions of any reference whatsoever to the points expected.[8]

This was removed; and in the next section but one, eventually entitled "Some Well-Meant Proposals for the Improvement of the Play," Shaw changed his opening sentence from "I have to thank a few American critics . . . for their heartfelt instructions as to how [the play] can be improved" to "I have to thank several critics on both sides of the Atlantic . . ."

Notwithstanding these cuts, the Preface was considerably more contentious than the play: indeed, the wave of adverse criticism which immediately followed publication can be traced in the main to Shaw's comments in the Preface. S. W. Dyde defends Shakespeare against Shaw;[9] John C. Blankenagel defends Schiller;[10] and while W. A. Oldfather disputes Joan's similarity to Socrates,[11] Arnold Lunn indignantly repudiates any connection between the Inquisition and the trial of Sir Roger Casement.[12] And in addition to critical articles, Shaw's play provoked at least two full-length books within a year of its appearance in print: Werner Jung's *La Jeanne d'Arc de Bernard Shaw*, which is highly adulatory; and J. M. Robertson's *Mr. Shaw and "The Maid,"* which is hostile to the point of hysteria.[13]

To many of his friends and acquaintances Shaw sent personal copies of his published play, some of them containing now well-known inscriptions. In the copy he sent to Dame Laurentia of Stanbrook Hall (the Benedictine convent in Worcestershire), with whom Shaw's friendship may be said to have been cemented by *Saint Joan*, he wrote "To Sister Laurentia from Brother Bernard." In T. E. Lawrence's copy he wrote "To Private Shaw from Public Shaw." The acknowledgements varied. Thomas Hardy's second wife, Florence, wrote to Shaw on 29 June 1924 to thank him for their copy, saying she had been reading it aloud to her husband: "Joan is now a real person to us. T.H. says he was never interested in her before."[14] John Drinkwater also sent praise for the play, though he found the supernatural part "vague and unconvincing."[15] And Laurence Binyon, gracefully acknowledging the copy Shaw sent to the British Museum, with remarkable unselfishness in view of his own unfinished attempt at a Joan play, commented, "I am glad to be contemporary with it, and rejoice in its success. I think you have done a great service to the cause of tragedy."[16]

Binyon here was initiating a debate which is as yet unfinished; a debate admirably summarized by Stanley Weintraub,[17] but a debate whose academic edges are frayed by an underlying possibility that a shift in critical consciousness has rendered almost obsolete the terms in which it is conducted. Moreover, the debate as to whether in *Saint Joan* Shaw has written a tragedy or not has not always been conducted at a convincing level. For Shaw himself it was "a tragedy as great as that of Prometheus."[18] Few have agreed. John C. Blankenagel disagrees that it is a tragedy at all, but his reasons are slight. Contrasting it to Schiller's *Die Jungfrau von Orleans* he claims that Schiller inclines more to tragic irony, pathos, and sentimentality, whereas Shaw's play contains more cynicism and comic byplay: "... he is fond of diatribe, raillery and comic elements ... Yet by their very abundance such elements are not conducive to maintaining *Saint Joan* on the level of high tragedy which its author claims for it."[19]

By contrast, Werner Jung claims that the essential irony of *Saint Joan* marks it out as a tragedy: "Ce qui est tragique, n'est pas qu'une femme ait été brulée, mais qu'elle l'ait été par des hommes qui croyaient, ce faisant, mériter de l'humanité."[20] For G. S. Fraser the play "fails to be a tragedy and becomes an inspirational pageant,"[21] though he does not explain why. For A. Obraztsova, "the tragedy of Joan is not so much her being burned alive. The tragedy above all is the impossibility of her resurrection either twenty-five years after her death or five hundred years later."[22] Richard Law also maintains that "Mr. Shaw has not made of Joan a figure of tragic appeal" and he does present a reason, which is that Joan is not, nor can be, the central figure in the play: "She bears to the rest of the play the relationship of the matchbox to the match which is struck upon it. The audience, realizing this, ceases to be interested in her, and becomes deeply interested in the characters with whom she is brought into contact."[23] And yet H. Lüdeke feels there is sufficient emphasis upon the protagonist to justify calling this play Shaw's "first and only tragedy," claiming that in it Shaw "reflected his own mental fate symbolically, as the great artist and world personage that he was, in a great figure of European history."[24]

The conflict is fully resolved by Louis L. Martz who squarely confronts the question: "Can a saint's play ever be truly tragic?" He recognizes the chief difficulty, previously propounded by S. H. Butcher, namely, that "the death of the martyr presents to us not the defeat but the victory of the individual; the issue of a conflict in which the individual is ranged on the same side as the higher powers, and the sense of suffering consequently lost in that of moral triumph."[25] To answer this difficulty, and bring *Saint Joan* within the scope of tragedy, Martz uses Joyce's comment on tragedy in *Portrait of the Artist*, claiming that tragedy demands a "human sufferer" and a "secret cause"—the former evoking pity, the latter, terror. The problem in the modern world is the absence of terror; or rather, in a history play, the difficulty of adjusting the ancient "secret cause" to the modern human sufferer. Martz goes on to claim that the peculiar power of *Saint Joan* (and *Murder in the Cathedral*) resides in the fact that "both Shaw and Eliot feel they cannot depend upon their audience to accept their saintly heroes as divinely inspired. The dramaturgy of both plays is based upon a deliberate manipulation of the elements of religious skepticism or uncertainty in the audience."[26] In this way, claims Martz, the saint may become a figure well adapted to arouse something very close to a tragic experience; by finding in the audience's uncertainty the "painful and pitiful aspects of experience that form the other side of the tragic tension."[27] Finally, Martz points out that "Joan and Beckett do not here represent humanity in the way of Hamlet or King Oedipus—by focusing within themselves the full tragic tension ... it is the whole fabric of the play that creates something like a tragic tension." The "hubris" is not Joan's, but Everyman's. The characters who "accuse Joan of pride and errors are in those accusations convicting themselves of the pride of self-righteousness and the errors of human certitude."[28] His argument presumably failed to convert Sylvan Barnet who, in 1956, published in *PMLA* an article called "Bernard Shaw on Tragedy." His argument is long and lucid, but contains some rather questionable assumptions which disqualify its conclusion. "Most teleological views," he claims, "are hostile to the idea of tragedy, for they see some great purpose in the bafflements and defeats which are the stuff of tragic drama." But in this sense Shaw's view was no more teleological than that of Sophocles, who presumably believed that the gods inflicted suffering upon men for their own inscrutable reasons. Shaw no more pretends to understand the Life Force which (he believes) motivates him and his creations than the Greeks did their gods, although Sophocles in the Theban Cycle seems to suggest that suffering leads to a greater awareness. With Joan, Oedipus might well cry "I am wiser now: and no one is any the worse for being wiser." Later Barnet claims that "*Saint Joan*, called by Shaw a tragedy, ... is at odds with the conventional tragic conception. Shaw refuses to admit that the movement of life (or at least, *a* movement) is from birth to death, and he insists on *going beyond* what is the *apparent* end."[29] As a matter of fact, Shakespeare (cited by Barnet as a writer of tragedies) is demonstrably more Christian than Shaw in his assumptions about the afterlife, and his tragedies abound in references to the beyond. Both Macbeth and Hamlet soliloquize on the subject; and although the latter sees death as "That bourne from which no traveller returns," a ghostly traveller *does* return from that bourne to give him the lie. There are many more ghosts in Shakespeare's tragedies than there are in *Saint Joan*.

Barnet then quotes Shaw's oft-quoted conversation with Paul Green:

> My plays are interludes between two realities and the meaning of them lies in what has preceded them and in what follows them. The beginning of one of my plays takes place exactly where an unwritten one ended. And the ending of my written play concludes where another play begins. It is the two unwritten plays they [the critics] should consider in order to get light on the one that lies between.[30]

Such a statement, claims Barnet, strikes at the very roots of tragedy, for tragedy depicts an action "which is 'complete,' but it is exactly such complete actions as the career, say, of Hamlet, that Shaw cannot abide." But Barnet's own statement is pure word-play. Tragedies are indeed "complete" actions; as, for example, *Oedipus Rex* is, although it is part of a trilogy: and Shaw's plays are every bit as "complete" as *Hamlet*, whose preceding play is "brought forward" and acted out by the players, while the play to come is left in the hands of Fortinbras.

It would be closer to the truth to say that Shaw's world of *becoming* rather than *being*, which naturally rejects a deterministic fatalism, and which culminates in his characters' awareness of future possibility rather than past failure, marks the difference between most of Shaw's plays and conventional tragedy. But on this point *Saint Joan* is uniquely enigmatic: the conclusion is at least doubtful as to the future; and the strong suggestion in the Epilogue is that if the events of Joan's life were to be repeated now, the end would be as inevitable. This circularity at least gives the play the force of a tragic satire, in which form the "conclusion" is often a reinforcement of the situation at the beginning, suggesting that the problem is unresolved. But the adjective, "tragic" is well applied, too. As Gerald Weales states: "For Shaw, of course, the tragedy is that the saints should have died at all, that their usefulness to the world should be destroyed by the world."[31] The irony of Joan's death in Shaw's play is intensified by the fact that the men who persecute or desert her are not villains, but fools: well-meaning, in some cases, but nevertheless narrow-minded fools. Nor does this militate against the play's tragic effect. S. John Macksoud and Ross Altman invoke Kenneth Burke on this point:

> Burke clarifies the suffusion of Shaw's high tragedy with this comic attitude: "The progress of humane enlightenment can go no further than in picturing people not as *vicious*, but as *mistaken*. When you add that people are *necessarily* mistaken, that *all* people are exposed to situations in which they must act as fools, that *every* insight contains its own special kind of blindness, you complete the comic circle, returning again to the lesson of humility that underlies great tragedy."[32]

Is such folly curable? That really is the force of Joan's final question. The positive implication is that under the influence of creative evolution, the world may be ready one day to receive God's saints; or as Frederic Wood puts it: "Gradually the mind of the human race is becoming emancipated; but there is need of many more Joans yet."[33] Binyon, then, was probably right in alluding to the service *Saint Joan* has performed to the cause of tragedy, not the least important aspect of which may well be the extension of our view of tragic form in the ways mentioned.

Now, according to Allardyce Nicoll, the remarkable thing about *Saint Joan* — which he considers together with Drinkwater's *Abraham Lincoln* — is that it had so *little* influence upon the drama that followed:

> In Drinkwater's *Abraham Lincoln* and Shaw's *Saint Joan* the English stage gave the world two dramas obviously inspired by the desire to use historical material for the purpose of illustrating a philosophy . . . the paradox enters in when we note that, despite the two great examples, English playwrights as a whole have not sought, when treating historical subjects, to make the past a commentary on the present.[34]

But, as I shall seek to prove, *Saint Joan* was influential beyond the boundaries of England, and even in England it had its effect, and comes near enough the beginning of the grand succession of history plays which form a pageant throughout the 1920s and thirties in the whole of Europe to make one suspect its influence at work.

Admittedly, its influence was observable at first in its immediate impact upon certain minor writers who saw fit to imitate Shaw.[35] One of these is worthy of mention. Frank Harris, in his *Unauthorised Biography* of Bernard Shaw, has a chapter entitled "The 'Saint Joan' Row." In it, after claiming (incorrectly) that he was the only discordant voice in the paeon of praise that greeted the publication of Shaw's play, he complains that Shaw has made the peasant girl into a "Shavian female," and a "too modern flapper." He further claims to know Joan at least as well as Shaw, stating that he had studied her life and personality for years, and, indeed, that he had written a play about her himself! In the spring of 1925, he claims, he sent Shaw a copy of *Joan La Romée*, as his play was called; and he quotes extensively from Shaw's reply (dated 20 May 1926). Shaw's reaction to Harris's play was totally predictable: it was useless of Harris to trespass on Shaw's domain:

> My making a drama of Joan outraged your instinct; you felt you must do something quite different with her; but you did not understand that the something was a short story and not another drama. The result is a shocking hybrid. Why not throw it into the fire and write your story? You have emptied out the Middle Ages and the Church and the Inquisition and the feudal system, and reduced the subject to a story of a young Virginian female, a few dullards, two crooks, and a very modern American executioner cheeking an English lord and snapping his fingers at the Holy Office (which would have burnt him in a brace of shakes for his heresy). Just like O. Henry, with the Harrisian style superimposed.[36]

His own intemperate response to the above, Harris quotes in full. Clearly wounded by Shaw's genial condescension, he blasts the notion that Joan was Shaw's property: "You talk of the 'ground' as being yours, and you would shoo me off this grass." But, he asserts, "I had written my play before I saw yours, and Joan had been in my head for twenty years with Jesus."[37] The letter, and later the chapter, conclude with a scathing attack upon Shaw's play. Normally a biographer gives himself the last word; but in Harris's case the proofs of his Shaw biography were seen through the press by Shaw himself; the subject surviving the biographer, who died on 26 August 1931. The job, as Shaw said, was one of the oddest he had ever had to do. Nevertheless, he seems to have done it with his usual thoroughness, resisting the temptation to defend himself or *Saint Joan*, merely adding a postscript to the book in which he states that he does not endorse Harris's comments. The postscript is dated 5 October 1931.

But a more amusing postscript to the "Saint Joan row" could have been written a month later, at which time Shaw received a letter from Lord Alfred Douglas (probably in response to the appearance of Harris's book) which states:

> I happened to be with him at the time he started to write his idiotic play about Joan of Arc. It is quite untrue that he wrote it (as he declares) before reading your own play. I was seeing him daily at the time (1925) at Nice. He

asked me all sorts of questions about Joan of Arc & about the Catholic attitude towards her which I answered to the best of my ability. He then told me that he was going to write a play about her which would "knock spots" off yours. I afterwards read the play and thought it beneath contempt. Not that I am such a very great admirer of your own play on the same subject. I take my Catholicism too seriously to approve of your flippant treatment of a martyr & Saint. But your play is of course brilliant & original whereas Harris's is simply the sort of thing a rather dull fifth form schoolboy might write.[38]

Far more significant was the impact of *Saint Joan* upon T. S. Eliot, who, having attacked Shaw's play when it first came out, went on to admit its influence upon him when he was writing *Murder in the Cathedral*. And even if, as Louis Crompton believes, that play can be regarded "as an attempt to reaffirm the ecclesiastical ideal of sainthood in reply to Shaw's challenge,"[39] as Martz points out, there are many correspondences of method which suggest that Eliot's dramaturgy owed much to that of Shaw: the "tone of satirical wit" that informs the two plays, the "realism" of Eliot's imagery, "frequent use in Part II of the recorded words that passed between Beckett and the Knights in the year 1170," and the "dim silence of the Cathedral setting."[40] And if one were to argue still that these are simply coincidental examples of Shaw and Eliot coming to similar terms with the modern consciousness, it is worth remarking that Shaw did so a full decade before Eliot.[41]

Saint Joan, as we have seen, was an international success in the 1920s, and this extended its influence to continental dramatists. Shaw's influence in the French theatre was slight before the famous Pitoëff production of *Saint Joan*, though this is not to deny some influence: Alfred Savoir was known as "the Bernard Shaw of the boulevards";[42] a critic has seen Shavian influence in Maeterlinck's *Le Miracle de Saint Antoine*[43] and even Anouilh, dividing his plays into *pièces roses* and *pièces noires*, appears to be echoing Shaw's *Plays Pleasant and Unpleasant*. But *Saint Joan* was a special case. Its effect on the Parisian public in 1925 has already been noted, though to this perhaps we should add its possible effect upon Ludmilla Pitoëff herself, who later experienced a religious crisis, "peut-être sous l'influence du rôle de Jeanne d'Arc, qu'elle interpreta long-temps."[44] But the play was to have a greater impact yet on the French public in 1940, at a time when "the people of Paris were cut off from help and hope" and "looking in vain for sustenance elsewhere, found it in the theatre."[45]

"The movement began," asserts Harold Hobson, "with Bernard Shaw,"[46] and he quotes from Beatrix Dussane's *Notes de théâtre*:

Plays about Joan of Arc deserve a prominent place in the long story of the struggle of the theatre with the censorship during the Occupation. In times when there was a scarcity of everything in Paris, it was almost enough to announce a production of *Joan of Arc* to obtain heat, raw materials, and costumes. Towards the end of 1940 Bernard Shaw's *Joan of Arc* [*Saint Joan*] was produced in this way. The German authorities thought they were being particularly clever, because it was a case of a French heroine fighting the English, and the author was the most troublesome of Irishmen. It was, in fact, a success that encouraged another company, in July 1941, to mount the *Jeanne d'Arc* of Péguy: that same *Jeanne* in which, a little later, writers in the clandestine Press were without difficulty to find admirable appeals to individual resistance.[47]

But it was not merely the uniquely French circumstances surrounding Joan of Arc which commended Shaw's play. *Saint Joan* is one of the first plays which, taking a well-known historical situation, dramatizes the confrontation between religious and political opponents. This point is made by Robert Cohen, who cites as an example of a similar play *Judith* by Jean Giraudoux.[48] During Giraudoux's formative years, French theatre directors in search of new writers were very favourably disposed to the work of Ibsen, Strindberg, Pirandello, and Shaw,[49] the Pitoëffs being a striking example. And in 1923, Louis Jouvet established himself at the Comédies des Champs-Elysées, where for two years his productions alternated with those of the Pitoëffs; the same Louis Jouvet who was later to interest himself almost exclusively in the work of Giraudoux. Cohen, while pointing out that Giraudoux was in ostensible reaction against the "drama of ideas," also remarks that "the structural form of Giraudoux's plays is dialectical as opposed to mimetic,"[50] and while one might demur to the extent of acknowledging Giraudoux's greater tendency than Shaw to embody or symbolize his debates, one could agree, I think, with Cohen's conclusion that "Giraudoux's drama owes a debt to Shaw which has never been properly calculated." It is not my purpose to calculate that debt here; merely to remark that a significant proportion of it, for the reasons given, must be owed to *Saint Joan*.

Another, and, from the standpoint of the development of later twentieth-century drama, more significant, continental dramatist whose debt to *Saint Joan* remains largely unexplored is Bertolt Brecht. Some of Shaw's influence on this writer clearly derives from plays written well before *Saint Joan* (Shaw's reputation having been more readily established in Germany than in France); and there is evidence that Brecht's directing techniques, simplicity of décor, and primitivized settings and costumes were well established before *Saint Joan* made them familiar to British and American audiences—at least by 1923, when Brecht directed his and Feuchtwanger's adaptation of Marlowe's *Edward II* at the Kammerspiele in Munich. But the following year Brecht came to Berlin. Much has been made of Pirandello's excited reaction to the first performance of *Saint*

Joan in New York; but considerably less has been deduced from the backstage presence of Brecht during the Berlin performance: "During his brief period as Dramaturg at the Deutsches Theatre (1924–1925) Brecht followed the rehearsals for Shaw's *Saint Joan* with extreme interest."[51] Also, John Fuegi reminds us that "G. B. Shaw and Frank Wedekind are consistently singled out for praise in Brecht's early critical writings. Both men, as Brecht himself acknowledged, profoundly influenced his views of the style and the function of the theatrical event in the twentieth century."[52] And elsewhere he expresses surprise that "inasmuch as the parallels with Shaw are striking and Brecht himself expressed fervent admiration for this socialist-polemicist-playwright, it is surprising that only one critic has, so far, studied the relationship between the plays and theater of these two men."[53] Again, such a task is well beyond the scope of this book. But it is worth commenting that Both Shaw and Brecht, in addition to being attracted to such themes as boxing, prostitution, and the Salvation Army, were also drawn to the new interpretation of old subjects, one of which was Saint Joan. Brecht used the story of Saint Joan three times: *Saint Joan of the Stockyards* (1929–31), *The Visions of Simone Machard* (1941–43), and an adaptation of Anna Segher's radio play *The Trial of Joan of Arc at Rouen, 1431* (1952). Comparing the first of these to Shaw's play, Schoep says that

> both Johanna and Saint Joan progress from naive belief to clear recognition; both become a threat to the ruling class through their activities, yet both are carefully used as pawns in the powerplay by those who are in control. Their real message to the world is drowned out by praise from those they criticize. However, there is neither romanticism nor one-sided propaganda. Both playwrights avoid painting in black and white: they recognize weaknesses in their "heroines," and human traits in their "villains." They also pursue a similar objective with their plays: they take the familiar subject of Joan of Arc in order to demonstrate the need for social change. Their interest in the topic of Joan of Arc reveals yet another similarity, namely their historical and dialectic approach in the tradition of Hegel and Marx. Hegel had pointed out that history advances through clashes of contradictory forces. Brecht and Shaw, who knew their Hegel well, illustrate these dialectics of progress in the conflict between Joan and the ruling classes.[54]

One remembers that the years from 1920 to 1930 were Brecht's most formative decade. *Saint Joan's* influence at such a time must have been profound. Schoep's concluding paragraph is worth quoting:

> We can be sure that Brecht was influenced by some aspects of Shaw's work, not in a narrow, positivistic sense, but in the form of catalytic impulses

originating from new and pioneering dramatic concepts. Although to a somewhat lesser extent than in the works of Wedekind, Kaiser or Shakespeare, Brecht found in the works of Bernard Shaw, a confirmation and a reinforcement of his own ideas about drama, particularly during the incubation period of his epic theatre.[55]

In short, to the direct influence of Shaw's play in the pre-war years upon British works as insignificant as *Charles the King* and as significant as *Murder in the Cathedral*, we must add its indirect influence via Brecht on postwar British drama, maintaining an unbroken line of descent from *Galileo* through Osborne's *Luther* to Bolt's *A Man for All Seasons*, of which Frank Granville Barker said that the author's dramatic purpose was to "do for Sir Thomas More what Shaw so magnificently did for Joan of Arc."[56]

In addition to the continuing effect of *Saint Joan* upon dramatists, is its influence upon the rest of the theatrical profession. Shaw's statement in the *Era* on 10 January 1934, was prophetic: "It is quite likely that sixty years hence, every great English and American actress will have a shot at 'St. Joan,' just as every great actor will have a shot at 'Hamlet.' . . . Plays which project great personalities will survive when much more profound and important topical plays—Ibsen's "Doll's House" for example—become quite obsolete." Certainly the list of actresses who have "had a shot" at Joan in the last half century is impressive, even if the aim of one or two has at times been off the target. The first decade of the play's existence was dominated by those actresses who had originally realized the part of Joan in their respective countries: Lenihan, Thorndike, Pitoëff, Bergner. By the thirties, other contenders were on the scene. Perhaps one of the finest Joans of that decade was Katharine Cornell in a production which "crowned the 1935–36 season in New York with great theatric grandeur." The *Stage* said:

> Miss Cornell's lyric and luminous Maid grows and glows with inner conviction and outward magnificence from the moment when, a laughing awkward peasant girl, she tumbles into de Baudricourt's presence at Vaucouleurs; through the young fire and inspiration of Chinon and Orleans; the triumph and lonely grandeur of Rheims; the long Gethsemane of Rouen; the rapt exaltation of the Princess of God.[57]

This production was also notable in having its remarkably fine sets designed by Jo Mielziner, who, one remembers, had played the Court Page in the New York première thirteen years previously. Shaw himself was greatly impressed by Miss Cornell when she called on him, describing her as "irresistible"; and in April 1940, when Langner wished to revive *Saint Joan*, using Katharine Hepburn in the lead, Shaw referred to the Cornell revival, saying "Is it not a bit soon to start a fresh tour of St. Joan on the heels of such a charmer?"[58]

Saint Joan may have been the first of his plays that Shaw ever considered for the screen; for as early as 1927 *Variety* reported that he was personally supervising screen tests of Sybil Thorndike, with the idea of sanctioning her appearance "in the picturization of his 'St. Joan,'" if the tests proved satisfactory. At this date none of Shaw's plays had been released for the screen. In fact, in that year the Cathedral Scene *was* filmed with Sybil Thorndike as the Maid, directed by Widgery Newman. Between 1934 and 1936 a full-length film was planned and Shaw produced a screenplay. In an edition of *Saint Joan* at present at Ayot St. Lawrence, Shaw has written in red ink on the title page, "Cut for Scenario Nov. 1934." At the end of the book his neat handwriting proclaims, "Roughly 35 pages cut out of 113—more than a third." The story of this ill-fated film has already produced one book[59] so there is no need to reproduce in print the fight with the Catholic Action Group of the Hays Office in Hollywood, which effectively put an end to the project. It is enough to recommend the book to the reader and to echo the author's view of the film that finally did emerge, seven years after Shaw's death, in which Graham Greene, perhaps unconsciously, satisfied the Catholic Action Group's objections by re-transferring the blame to the minor clerics who conducted the trial and removing the secular interpretation of the miracles.

Although the play was never made into a film in Shaw's lifetime, the first radio production of *Saint Joan* took place in 1941, with Constance Cummings as the Maid. Her performance, described by Val Gielgud as "notably brilliant," also made radio history as it was given without a script. Another notable "first" about this production was the fact that Shaw for the first time "showed a tendency to withdraw from his absolute standpoint. He admitted that certain references, such as those to the Visions in the last act, could have been cut as being aurally ineffective, and that certain other emendations—which he specified—in the text would have been desirable."[60] St. John Ervine wrote to Shaw the following day to express his delight in the production, adding, "The play is indestructible. No one by miscasting or bad production, can destroy or even injure it."[61] Although this opinion was not shared by L. C. Lloyd of the *Spectator*, who when Constance Cummings repeated her radio performance in 1947 complained that she had hardly a glimmer of the spirituality which the real Joan must have possessed,[62] the truth of St. John Ervine's comment gradually established itself as the premières faded from public memory. As the critic of *Theatre World* put it the following year: "With each new production of Shaw's great play it becomes manifest that there are a dozen interpretations to the title role."[63] For this critic the acting of Celia Johnson held "the ring of truth before all others,"[64] in a splendid revival which featured Bernard Miles as de Baudricourt, John Clements as Dunois, and Alec Guinness as the dauphin.

And so it has been ever since. Since Shaw's death in November 1950 there have been many revivals of *Saint Joan* in London, starring actresses of widely divergent talents. One thinks of the brilliant performances of Siobhann McKenna and Barbara Jefford in the fifties, of Joan Plowright and Judi Dench in the sixties, and of Angela Pleasance, Julia Foster, and Eileen Atkins in the seventies. And the play's universal appeal was again demonstrated when in the fifties it proved to be the greatest box-office success in the stage history of Israel, with Orna Porath's performance at the Chamber Theatre.

Although Shaw did not consider *Saint Joan* his best play (preferring *Heartbreak House*), he was privately pleased by its enthusiastic reception; and in 1925 when he received the Nobel Prize for literature, there can be little doubt that *Saint Joan* was regarded by the selection committee as Shaw's crowning achievement.[65] Though he went on to write more plays, including *The Apple Cart* and *In Good King Charles's Golden Days*, none of them measured up to its greatness. And no other play of his attracted the same attention from the masses: "...Shaw did not really capture the ordinary man and woman until 'St Joan' appeared in 1924. The speech of the Inquisitor and the words of the Saint touched mind and heart alike. He was then 67 and the worship of Shaw began. Barrie called him 'our only angel.' Shaw complained that criticism was being overtaken by reverence."[66]

In retrospect, it seems that Shaw's encounter with Joan of Arc made as lasting an impression upon him as it did upon his critics. In a stained-glass window of the West London Ethical Church, Shaw appears with Anatole France, and Joan of Arc stands between them. And in Shaw's garden at Ayot St. Lawrence, a sculpture of the Maid, by his neighbour Clare Winsten, was placed in his ninetieth year. Just before his last illness, Shaw described it:

> Down in the dell and westward veering
> You see the Maid of Orleans peering
> For British foes...[67]

He was very fond of this statue, reports his secretary Blanche Patch, because it depicted Joan as a peasant woman, and not "dressed in armour like a film star." But more than mere fondness is implied in Shaw's will, which directed that his ashes, mixed with those of his wife, who had predeceased him by seven years and who had played more than her usual part in bringing *Saint Joan* about, should be scattered at the foot of her whose own ashes were cast into the Seine five hundred and nineteen years before.

Notes

Chapter 1

1. T. Michael Pope, "The Solitude of the Saint," *Outlook* 53 (5 April 1924): 235
2. Luigi Pirandello, "Pirandello Distills Shaw," *New York Times Magazine*, 13 January 1924, sec. IV, p. 1. Of course, the last thing that Shaw wanted his plays to produce was an acceptance of the status quo: Saint Joan's question which concludes the play may be anguished, but it is not rhetorical.
3. G. K. Chesterton, "Chesterton Surveys Shaw at 70," *New York Times Magazine*, 25 July 1926, p. 1.
4. See, for example, W. Y. Tindall, *Forces in Modern British Literature 1885–1956* (New York: Vintage Books, 1956); Julian Kaye, *Bernard Shaw and the Nineteenth-Century Tradition* (Norman: University of Oklahoma Press, 1958); and J. Percy Smith, *The Unrepentant Pilgrim: A Study of the Development of Bernard Shaw* (Toronto: Macmillan, 1965).
5. See Stanley Weintraub, *Journey to Heartbreak* (New York: Weybright and Talley, 1971), p. 247.
6. See, for example, Edmund Wilson, "Bernard Shaw Since the War," *New Republic* 40 (27 August 1924): 381; and Margery Morgan's brilliant analysis of this play in *The Shavian Playground: An Exploration of the Art of Bernard Shaw* (London: Methuen, 1972).
7. In this connection, Shaw wrote to Lady Gregory, on 19 August 1909:

> All this problem of the origin of evil, the mystery of pain, and so forth does not puzzle me. My doctrine is that God proceeds by the method of trial and error just like a workman perfecting an aeroplane. . . . To me the sole hope of human salvation lies in teaching Man to regard himself as an experiment in the realization of God, to regard his hand as God's hand, his brain as God's brain, his purpose as God's purpose. He must regard God as a helpless longing which longed him into existence by its desperate need for an executive organ. You will find it all in *Man and Superman*, as you will find it all behind *Blanco Posnet*. (British Library Add. MSS. 50534)

8. Shaw described this play as "historical tragedy at its deepest: a point reached only by religious persecution," in a letter to Katherine Gatch, who quotes it in her article, "The Real Sorrow of Great Men," *College English*, February 1947, p. 237. See also John Mason Brown, "The Prophet and the Maid," *Saturday Review of Literature* 34 (27 October 1951): 28; rpt. in *"Saint Joan" Fifty Years After*, ed. Stanley Weintraub (Baton Rouge: Louisiana State University Press, 1973).

9. William James, *The Varieties of Religious Experience* (New York: Longman, Green and Co., 1929), p. 499.

10. See "What is My Religious Faith?" in *Sixteen Self-Sketches* (London: Constable and Co., 1949).

11. Susan C. Stone, "Shaw's Heroic Model in Flux: From Caesar to Charles," *English Studies in Canada* 2, no. 3 (Fall 1976): 310.

12. Gatch, "Great Men," p. 237.

13. Jack Crawford, "Broadway Is Inspired," *Drama*, 14 February 1924, p. 179.

14. William Archer to Shaw, 22 June 1921, British Library Add. MSS. 50528, vol. 21.

15. The Rev. Joseph Leonard, C.M. (1877–1964) was ordained in 1902, did scholastic work at St. Vincent's, Castleknock, All Hallows, Dublin, and St. Mary's Training College, Hammersmith, London, England, where Shaw corresponded with him in 1922 and 1923. He was the author of *Saint Vincent de Paul and Mental Prayer*, and translator of Abbé Huvelin's *Some Spiritual Guides of the XVIIIth Century*, Lavedan's *Heroic Life of St. Vincent de Paul*, Hoornaert's *Saint Teresa in Her Writings*, and Père Coste's *Life and Works of St. Vincent de Paul*. He also translated and edited *The Letters of St. Vincent de Paul*.

16. See James A. Costello, "The Rev. Joseph Leonard, C.M.," *All Hallows Annual 1966* (Dublin), p. 145.

17. Denis Gwynn, "Now and Then," *Cork Examiner*, 2 November 1964.

18. Ibid., 21 June 1966.

19. According to the Rev. Kevin Condon, C.M., archivist of All Hallows, Dublin, in a letter to the author, 14 February 1978.

20. See Gwynn, "Now and Then."

21. No doubt the book he read was Cyril Martindale's *Charles Dominic Plater, S.J.*, which came out in that year.

22. Leonard to Shaw, 14 December 1922, British Library Add. MSS. 50518. "Queer fish" is precisely what Shaw calls Saint Joan in the opening paragraph of the Preface to his play.

23. Leonard to Shaw, 14 December 1922, ibid. His first reference is to J. E. J. Quicherat, *Procès de Jeanne d'Arc*, 5 vols. (Paris: J. Renouard, 1841), and *Aperçus Nouveaux* (Paris: J. Renouard, 1850). The translation by T. Douglas Murray is entitled *Jeanne d'Arc, Maid of Orleans, Deliverer of France; Being the Story of Her Life, Her Achievements, and Her Death, as attested on Oath and Set forth in the Original Documents* (London: William Heinemann, 1902).

24. Cockerell to Shaw, 4 March 1945, British Library Add. MSS. 50531.

25. Archibald Henderson, *George Bernard Shaw: Man of the Century* (New York: Appleton-Century-Crofts, 1956), p. 599.

26. Norman Carrington, *Notes on Chosen English Texts* (London: James Brodie, 1950), p. 20.

27. F. S. Boas, "Joan of Arc in Shakespeare, Schiller and Shaw," *Shakespeare Quarterly* 2 (January 1951): 42.

28. Brown, "The Prophet and the Maid," p. 27.

29. Blanche Patch, *Thirty Years with G.B.S.* (London: Victor Gollancz, 1951), p. 44.

30. St. John Ervine, *Bernard Shaw: His Life, Work and Friends* (London: Constable and Co., 1956), p. 496.

31. Lawrence Langner, *G.B.S. and the Lunatic* (London: Hutchinson, 1964), p. 57.

32. J. W. Miller, *Modern Playwrights at Work* (New York: Samuel French, 1968), p. 184.

33. G. B. Shaw, "The Ten Birthplaces of *Saint Joan*," *Irish Independent* (Dublin), 13 November 1943.

34. G. B. Shaw, "Shaw Unperturbed by Immortality," replies to a questionnaire by Leslie Rees, *Era* (London), 10 January 1934.
35. Patch, *Thirty Years*, p. 45.
36. Lillah McCarthy was the actress who created the first generation of Shavian heroines at the Court Theatre. By 1923 she was Lady Keeble, having taken a second husband (her first had been the actor Harley Granville-Barker), and lived in a large house at Boar's Hill, three miles outside Oxford, where her husband lectured.
37. G. B. Shaw, *To a Young Actress: The Letters of Bernard Shaw to Molly Tompkins*, ed. Peter Tompkins (New York: Clarkson N. Potter, 1960), p. 42. Molly Tompkins was an actress born in New York and educated in Georgia. Together with her sculptor husband, she went to London in 1921 with the express purpose of seeking out Bernard Shaw and developing a Shaw Theatre. On Shaw's advice she enrolled in the Royal Academy of Dramatic Arts, and she and her husband became fast friends and travelling companions of the dramatist until the latter's death.
38. Quoted in Langner, *G.B.S.* p. 89.
39. G. B. Shaw, "Playhouses and Plays," rpt. in *Shaw on Theatre*, ed. E. J. West (New York: Hill and Wang, 1958), pp. 180–81. The article makes frequent reference to Shakespeare, appropriately enough, since the Shaws were in Shakespeare country; and Shaw's manuscript of *Saint Joan* is originally divided into five acts, which are subdivided into Shakespearean scenes.
40. Shaw, *To a Young Actress*, p. 45.
41. Originally Act III, sc. 1: a Shakespearian division perhaps suggested by his trip to Stratford-on-Avon.
42. Originally Act III, sc. 2.
43. Originally Act III, sc. 3.
44. Originally Act IV.
45. See pp. 17–19 for an account of this most interesting Fabian.
46. Shaw to Mary Hankinson, 17 August 1923, in the possession of Mr. Philip Goode of Didcot, England.
47. Shaw, *To a Young Actress*, p. 49.
48. G. B. Shaw, comment made on p. ii of the notebook containing the original shorthand draft of *Saint Joan*.
49. Shaw, *To a Young Actress*, p. 52.

Chapter 2

1. Quoted by Sybil Thorndike in R.J. Minney, *Recollections of George Bernard Shaw* (Englewood Cliffs: Prentice-Hall, 1969), p. 111.
2. A. Russell Thorndike, *Sybil Thorndike* (London: Butterworth, 1929), p. 291.
3. Quoted by Sybil Thorndike in H. Pearson, *Bernard Shaw: His Life and Personality* (London: Collins, 1942), p. 377.
4. Thorndike, *Sybil Thorndike*, p. 290.
5. Sheridan Morley, *Sybil Thorndike: A Life in the Theatre* (London: Weidenfeld and Nicolson, 1977), p. 73.
6. Review of "The Cenci," *The Times* (London), 14 November 1922, p. 8c.
7. See Stanley Weintraub, "Bernard Shaw's Other Saint Joan," *Shavian* 2, no. 10 (October 1964), pp. 7–13; rpt. in *"Saint Joan" Fifty Years After*, ed. S. Weintraub.
8. St. John Ervine, *Bernard Shaw: His Life, Work and Friends* (London: Constable and Co., 1956), p. 49. Mary Hankinson was fifty-five.
9. "Model Woman," *Daily Mirror* (London), 29 November 1950.

10. "Miss Mary Hankinson," ibid., 2 December 1952.
11. See the Fabian Society Papers at Nuffield College: H 37/2 ff. 115, 116.
12. See B. Drake and M. Cole, eds., *Our Partnership*, by Beatrice Webb (London: Longmans, Green and Co., 1948), p. 508.
13. According to John Parker, M.P., in a letter to Miss R. Howard, 9 May 1976 (in possession of the author).
14. Fabian Society Papers: G 24/10 ff. 8–12.
15. Ibid.
16. Ibid.
17. Ibid.
18. G.R.B.W., "Hanky," *Fabian News* 63, no. 12 (January 1953): 1.
19. Rev. F. J. Hankinson, address at Mary Hankinson's funeral: insert in *Ling Monthly*, December 1952.
20. Ibid.
21. "Model Woman," *Daily Mirror* (London), 20 November 1950.
22. Quoted from the *English Review* in the *New York Times*, 19 September 1926, in answer to Sarolea's article "Has Mr. Shaw Understood Joan of Arc?" *English Review*, August 1926, pp. 175–82.
23. This interview was published under the title "Bernard Shaw Talks of His *Saint Joan*" in *Literary Digest International Book Review* the following March.
24. Jules Michelet, *Histoire de France* (Brussels: L. Hauman, 1834); *Jeanne d'Arc* formed part of volume 5 and was republished in 1853 with some modifications as a separate work.
25. Henri Wallon, *Jeanne d'Arc* (Paris: Hachette, 1860).
26. Henri Martin, *Jeanne d'Arc* (Paris: Furne, 1857).
27. He saw it in May 1907.
28. See *Bernard Shaw and Mrs. Patrick Campbell: Their Correspondence*, ed. Alan Dent (London: Victor Gollancz, 1952), p. 163.
29. There are of course numerous other books at Shaw's Corner which deal with the life of the saint, but most of them are post 1923; even Shaw's personal copy of Gabriel Hanoteaux's *Jeanne d'Arc* (1911), for example, is dated February 1925.
30. Archibald Henderson, "George Bernard Shaw Self-Revealed," *Fortnightly Review* 1 April 1926, p. 438.
31. This age was later changed to "17 or 18."
32. Shaw always took immense care with the physical descriptions of his characters; and one reason (rarely mentioned) was his interest in physiognomy. One has only to read his reviews of Francis Werner's *Physical Expression* and Rosa Baughan's *Handbook of Physiognomy* in the *Pall Mall Gazette* in 1885 or to notice the prevailing facial characteristics of certain of his principal figures to realize this: for example, Saint Joan shares her "resolute mouth" with Sartorius, Morell, and Blanco Posnet; and "spreading nostrils" are a sign of determination.
33. W. Tittle, "Mr. Bernard Shaw Talks about *St. Joan*," *Outlook* (New York) 137 (25 June 1924): 311–13; rpt. in *"Saint Joan" Fifty Years After*, ed. S. Weintraub.
34. He visited Orleans in 1913.
35. T. Douglas Murray, ed. and trans., *Jeanne d'Arc, Maid of Orleans, Deliverer of France, Being the Story of Her Life, Her Achievements, and Her Death, as Attested on Oath and Set forth in the Original Documents* (London: William Heinemann, 1902). Hereafter, this work will be cited as Murray.
36. Murray, p. 229.

37. Ibid., p. 37.
38. T. Michael Pope, "The Solitude of the Saint," *Outlook* 53 (5 April 1924): 235.
39. Murray, p. 294.
40. L. Alma Tadema to Shaw, British Library Add. MSS. 50519, vol. 22.
41. G. B. Shaw, "Note by the Author," program of the New Theatre London, 26 March 1924.
42. Christopher Hollis, "Some Notes on Mr. Shaw's *St. Joan,*" *Dublin Review* 82 (April 1928): 177–88.
43. Anatole France, *The Life of Joan of Arc*, trans. Winifred Stephens, 2 vols. (London: John Lane, 1908), 2: 137.
44. Zdeněk Vančura, "The Dramatic Structure of G. B. Shaw's *Saint Joan,*" *Časopis Pro Moderní Filologii* 40 (1958): 17–18.
45. Stanley Solomon, "*Saint Joan* as Epic Tragedy," *Modern Drama*, February 1964, p. 441
46. Louis Crompton, *Shaw the Dramatist* (Lincoln: University of Nebraska Press, 1969), p. 198.
47. In E. Cobham Brewer's *A Dictionary of Miracles, Imitative, Realistic and Dogmatic* (Philadelphia: J. B. Lippincott Company, 1966), no less than twenty-six saints are credited with the power of multiplying food, including St. Brigit of Kildare, who caused a dry cow to give three pailsful of milk.
48. Shaw clarified this in his letter to Lawrence Langner (reprinted in the latter's *The Magic Curtain* [New York: Dutton, 1951], p. 182) after he had seen photographs of the Theatre Guild's production: "The steward should not be a zany, but a respectable elderly man whom nobody nowadays would dream of assaulting. Otherwise B's handling of him becomes mere knockabout farce."
49. Murray, p. 229
50. William Archer to Shaw, 12 June 1923, British Library Add. MSS. 50528, vol. 21.
51. From France's *Life of Joan of Arc*, if from nowhere else, Shaw could have learned of the contemporary verse drama of over 20,000 lines entitled *Le Mystère de siège*, the siege in question being that of Orleans, with the Maid for its heroine; and among the speaking personages in the work, appears the Maréchal de Rais. Anatole France expresses mild astonishment that the infamous "Vampire of Machecoul," Bluebeard, should be represented as fighting alongside the Maid for the deliverance of Orleans!
52. See his letter to Mark Twain, 3 July 1907, in *Bernard Shaw: Collected Letters, 1898–1910*, ed. Dan H. Laurence (London: Max Reinhardt, 1972), p. 696.
53. Samuel Clemens, *Personal Recollections of Joan of Arc by the Sieur Louis de Conte, her page and secretary. Freely translated out of the ancient French into modern English from the original unpublished manuscript in the National Archives of France by Jean François Alden*. Edited (or rather written) by Mark Twain (London: Chatto and Windus, 1896), p. 92. Michelet also describes the Archbishop as an "old fox." So do Bluebeard and La Trémouille in Shaw's play.
54. France, *Joan of Arc*, p. 152.
55. Shaw had used this very form of words in his opening scene, when Poulengy had said: "The dauphin is in Chinon like a rat in a corner except that he won't fight."
56 Clemens, *Personal Recollections*, p. 93.
57. Murray, p. 282.
58. But whereas Mackaye bases his set on the available facts, Shaw does not: at the time that *Jeanne d'Arc* was written, the remains of the actual chamber where Joan met the Dauphin still existed, described by Andrew Lang as "a roofless ruin . . . a wall with the wide fireplace still intact." Accordingly, Mackaye's throne chamber includes this fire-

place and its chimney seat. Shaw, on the other hand, appears to have been influenced again by Mark Twain, who describes the setting for the meeting as follows: "There was a wide free space down the middle of the hall, and at the end of it was a throne royally canopied, and upon it sat a crowned and sceptred figure nobly clothed and blazing with jewels." Shaw's original manuscript pictured the room thus: "Throne appears on the right: a narrow chair raised on a dais of two steps with a canopy all of carved wood. Bluebeard is standing theatrically on the dais, playing the king. . . . The door, guarded by two men-at-arms, is opposite the throne at the other side of the room; and a clear path from one to the other is being kept and lined by the courtiers."

59. Percy Mackaye, *Jeanne d'Arc: A Drama in Verse* (New York: Macmillan, 1906), p. 63.
60. Murray, p. 28.
61. Robert Southey, *Joan of Arc, an Epic Poem* (London: Longman, 1853), pp. 44–45.
62. Mackaye, *Jeanne d'Arc*, pp. 76–77.
63. Shaw's scepticism here may be well-founded; but he makes no mention of Joan's previous claim to have recognized Robert de Baudricourt, although she had never seen him: "I knew him, thanks to my voice, which made me recognize him." Murray, p. 11.
64. France, *Joan of Arc*, p. 170.
65. "Mr. Hornblow Goes to the Play," *Theatre Magazine* 39 (March 1924): 16. J. van Kan a year later also takes issue with what he calls "the caricaturing of the king." In particular he objects, on historical grounds, to the disrespectful way Charles is treated by his court, and by the public statements about his legitimacy. In addition, he queries the line "If we go to Rheims and have a coronation, Anne will want new dresses," asking "Who is Anne? . . . the Queen of France was called Marie (of Anjou); and in 1492 no one but the Queen had any right to clothes at the King's expense." J. van Kan, "Bernard Shaw's *Saint Joan*: An Historical Point of View," *Fortnightly Review* 108 (July 1925): 39; rpt. in *"Saint Joan" Fifty Years After*, ed. S. Weintraub.
66. Clemens, *Personal Recollections*, pp. 124–25.
67. Originally, Act III, sc. i.
68. Mrs. Florence Caddy, *In the Footsteps of Jeanne d'Arc; a Pilgrimage* (London: Hurst and Blackett, 1886), pp. 11–12.
69. Sir Sydney Cockerell to Shaw, 4 March 1945, British Library Add. MSS. 50531, vol. 24.
70. Hideo Takeuchi, "Saint Joan," *Humanities* (Yokohama), September 1956, p. 5.
71. Though in his testimony, Dunois claimed that he replied simply, "Yes."
72. Murray, p. 232.
73. .This may have been one of the excisions Shaw was referring to when he told Henderson: "In my enthusiasm I put into my play many interesting historical incidents. But when the proofs came to me, I found that many of these incidents, while enormously interesting in themselves, were imperfectly related to the dramatic action. So I am now engaged in a drastic revision of the proofs." "Bernard Shaw Talks of His *Saint Joan*," *Literary Digest International Book Review* 2 (March 1924): 286.

Chapter 3

1. In the manuscript, Act III, sc. ii.
2. These characters all appear in the First Part of Shakespeare's *Henry VI*.
3. In the shorthand version he is described as "verging on middle age." Cauchon speaks of the death of John Huss (1415) as "thirteen years ago." Richard de Beauchamp, Earl of Warwick, was born in 1382.

4. J. van Kan, "Bernard Shaw's *Saint Joan*: An Historical Point of View," *Fortnightly Review* 108 (July 1925). Van Kan is incorrect as to the date.

5. Desmond MacCarthy, *New Statesman*, 5 April 1924.

6. G. B. Shaw, "Note" by the author from the program of the New Theatre, London. In Murray, p. 186, we read: "There was a short interval in which an Englishman addressed the Bishop as a traitor, to which he answered that he lied."

7. M. A. Cohen, "The 'Shavianization' of Cauchon," *Shaw Review* 20, no. 2 (May 1977): 63.

8. Ibid., p. 64.

9. Ibid., p. 65. My italics.

10. G. B. Shaw, *The Quintessence of Ibsenism* in *Major Critical Essays* (London: Constable and Co., 1932), p. 42.

11. Arthur Mizener, "Poetic Drama and the Well-Made Play," *English Institute Essays* (1949), p. 46.

12. G. Buchmann, *Geflügelte Worte* (1898), quoted in the *Oxford Dictionary of Quotations*, 2nd ed. (London: Oxford University Press, 1966), p. 266. Interestingly, Cauchon's reference to Huss, earlier in the scene, was originally incomplete. Shaw's shorthand reads:

    The man Huss, burned only   ago at   infected all Bohemia with it. (fol. 29)

    Shaw, in researching to fill the gap for the number of years and the place may well have come across the account of Huss' last words, and added them to finish the scene at that time.

13. Originally Act III, sc. iii.

14. At least one critic deplored this omission. Zdeněk Vančura in "The Dramatic Structure of *Saint Joan*," *Časopis Pro Moderní Filologii* 40 (1958): 18, complains of "the weakest point in Shaw's play; his heroine never appears as a leader of men. We do not see her—in the third act—at the head of the French army."

15. Murray, p. xv.

16. Ibid.

17. Of course, this is not merely a glimpse of the fighting tactics of fourteenth-century France; it also presages Joan's capture.

18. It is the only evidence preserved in the original French.

19. Murray, p. 280.

20. Samuel Clemens, *Personal Recollections of Joan of Arc* (London: Chatto and Windus, 1896), p. 204.

21. Murray, p. 220

22. Ibid., p. 22.

23. Percy Mackaye, *Jeanne d'Arc: A Drama in Verse* (New York: Macmillan, 1906), p. 30.

24. During the "Nine Private Examinations," Jeanne testified about her voices as follows: "Before the raising of the Siege of Orleans and every day since, when they speak to me, they call me often, 'Jeanne the Maid; Daughter of God.'" Murray, p. 64.

25. Father Joseph Leonard to Shaw, British Library Add. MSS. 50519, vol. 22. (Leonard had presumably returned to England ahead of Shaw.) His research did not prevent R. Ellis Roberts from complaining that the "angelus" reference was an anachronism: "[the angelus was] a devotion...invented by Pope Alexander VI, who was born the year Joan was murdered." Review of first English production in the *Bookman*, May 1924.

26. F. Trajanowa to Shaw, 29 October 1921, British Library Add. MSS. 50518, vol. 11.

27. J. Rosselli, "The Right Joan and the Wrong One," *Twentieth Century*, April 1955, pp. 375–79.
28. Ibid., p. 378.
29. "Nine Private Examinations," Murray, pp. 65–66.
30. J. E. J. Quicherat, *Aperçus Nouveaux* (Paris: J. Renouard, 1850), p. 5.
31. Robert Southey, *Joan of Arc, an Epic Poem* (London: Longman, 1853), p. 18.
32. Clemens, *Personal Recollections*, p. 3.
33. *The Collected Works of Henrik Ibsen*, trans. William Archer (New York: Charles Scribner's Sons, 1923), 3: 215–16.
34. G. B. Shaw, *The Quintessence of Ibsenism*, p. 75.
35. Many critics, among them J. P. Hackett, S. I. Hsiung, C. E. M. Joad, and R. M. Ohmann have seen in his saint a partial picture of Shaw himself.

Chapter 4

1. Originally Act IV.
2. And Murray in his Introduction (p. xxii) says "The trial is one of the most enthralling dramas in all history."
3. John Mason Brown, "The Prophet and the Maid," *Saturday Review of Literature* (New York) 34 (27 October 1951): 28.
4. A. Lunn, "The Inquisition and Mr. G. Bernard Shaw," *Review of the Churches* 3, n.s. (January 1926): 77
5. Christopher Hollis, "Some Notes on Mr. Shaw's *St. Joan*," *Dublin Review* 82 (April 1928): 181.
6. *New Criterion* 4 (April 1926): 389–90.
7. G. B. Shaw, from the program of the New Theatre.
8. J. H. Buckland, "Saint Joan," *History*, January 1925, p. 286
9. Nicolas Loyseleur was "a familiar of my Lord of Beauvais," according to Guillaume Manchon, at the first enquiry in 1449, who further reports that he "pretended that he belonged to the Maid's country; by this means he found a way to have speech and familiar converse with her, telling her news of her country that would please her. He asked to be her confessor, and of what she told him privately he found means to inform the Notaries: indeed, at the beginning of the Trial, I and Boisguillaume, with witnesses, were put secretly in an adjoining room, where there was a hole through which we could hear, in order that we might report what she said to Loyseleur. As I think, what the Maid said or stated familiarly to Loyseleur he reported to the Notaries; and from this were made memoranda for questions in the Trial, to find some way of catching her unawares." Murray, p. 165. Manchon also explains (ibid, p. 166) the sound reasons given by Lohier as to why the "Process" was of no value: it lacked the form of an ordinary trial: it was carried on in a shut-up place where those concerned were unable to speak freely; that it dealt with the honour of the King of France, yet he had not been called, nor any who were for him; that it lacked legal documents and articles which would guide the accused to answer the Masters and Doctors on the great matters involved.
10. This information originates in Murray, p. 159, where Brother Ysambard de la Pierre claims that for having told Jeanne about the Council of Basle, "on account of these things and many others, the English and their officers threatened me terribly, so that, had I not kept silence, they would have thrown me into the Seine."
11. This alteration in wording from "mercy" to "justice" seems to me significant.

12. Murray, p. 94; and also see Appendix to Murray, p. 341. For some reason Shaw changes the original number of articles to 64.
13. Murray, p. 111.
14. Ibid., pp. 66, 168–69, 182.
15. William Searle, "Shaw's Saint Joan as 'Protestant,'" *Shaw Review* 15, no. 3 (September 1972): 114.
16. One of those who saw Shaw's play as a sort of "apology for the Inquisition" was Dean Inge, the Dean of St. Paul's, who said in a newspaper article on 12 January 1928: "I don't suppose he is serious. It amuses him to pretend that the modern Englishman, who is the most sentimentally humane man on earth at heart, is no better than Torquemada." Shaw replied, characteristically, that his play contained not an apology for the Inquisition, but "the official stock case for the Inquisition star chamber, the Consistorial Courts, the Anti-Blasphemy Act and the general medical counsel [sic] which at least keeps up the Torquemada tradition by trying to prevent the administration of chloroform to the patients of medical heretics." "Shaw Turns Wrath Against Dean Inge," *New York Times*, 14 January 1928, p. 5:6.
17. Samuel Clemens, *Personal Recollections of Joan of Arc* (London: Chatto and Windus, 1896), p. 349.
18. Murray, p. 254.
19. The height of the keep is mentioned in Murray, p. 337.
20. Murray, p. 18.
21. Shaw had made this point in Scene I, through the mouth of de Baudricourt. This information was available in many of his sources; and also in Simeon Luce, *Jeanne d'Arc à Domrémy. recherches critiques sur les origines de la mission de la Pucelle* (Paris: 1886).
22. Murray, p. 103.
23. Originally this speech was given to the Inquisitor, but transposed to Cauchon for obvious reasons.
24. R. Ellis Roberts, "*Saint Joan* by Bernard Shaw. At the New Theatre," *Bookman*, May 1924, p. 140.
25. Shaw changed the tense from present to imperfect, and added the sentence "I am a prisoner guarded by soldiers," to fit the reality of Joan's situation.
26. Murray, p. 136.
27. Ibid., p. 130n.
28. Shaw was probably also influenced here by the Latin account quoted in Murray, "Johanna, timens ignem, dixit se velle obedire ecclesiae."
29. Murray, p. 203.
30. Clemens, *Personal Recollections*, p. 409.
31. Murray, p. 133.
32. J. M. Robertson, in *Mr. Shaw and "The Maid"* (London: Richard Cobden-Sanderson, 1925), for example, and Arnold Lunn.
33. J. Percy Smith, *The Unrepentant Pilgrim* (Toronto: Macmillan, 1965), p. 19.
34. Murray, p. 255.
35. Ibid., p. 138.
36. Desmond MacCarthy speaking of Shaw's *Getting Married* in *Theatre* (London: MacGibbon & Kee, 1954), p. 40.
37. Robert Southey, *Joan of Arc, an Epic Poem* (London: Longman, 1853), p. 22.
38. J. Rosselli, "The Right Joan and the Wrong One," *Twentieth Century*, April 1955, p. 382.

39. Originally "drag" her out.
40. His evidence is to be found on pp. 301–2 of Murray.
41. The court of the bailiff.
42. Later the words "the most" were replaced by "an."
43. The phrase "not the guilty" was removed during revision.
44. Murray, p. 161.
45. Ibid., pp. 175–76.
46. Later, Shaw transposed the words "bone" and "hair."
47. Shaw changed "sir," to "my lord," which again heightens the moment.
48. Murray, p. 162.

Chapter 5

1. Jack Crawford, "Broadway Is Inspired," *Drama*, 14 February 1924, p. 179.
2. J. L. Kimball, "The Epilogue to St. Joan," *Spectator*, 31 January 1925, p. 156.
3. R. Ellis Roberts, "*Saint Joan* by Bernard Shaw. At the New Theatre," *Bookman*, May 1924, p. 140.
4. Reginald Owen, "Tragedy, Comedy and Farce," *Drama* (New York) 15, no. 3 (December 1924): 1.
5. Helen MacAfee, "Saint Joan and Other Plays," *Yale Review* 14 (January 1925) 388.
6. Harold Kellock, "A Saint Militant," *Freeman* (New York) 8 (16 January 1924): 448.
7. E. J. West, "*Saint Joan*: A Modern Classic Reconsidered," *Quarterly Journal of Speech* 40, no. 3 (October 1954): 254 rpt. in *"Saint Joan" Fifty Years After*, ed. S. Weintraub.
8. A. N. Kaul, "George Bernard Shaw: From Anti-Romance to Pure Fantasy," *The Action of English Comedy: Studies in the Encounter of Abstraction and Experience from Shakespeare to Shaw* (New Haven: Yale University Press, 1970), pp. 323–24.
9. Shaw, from the Program of the New Theatre.
10. G. B. Shaw, *Bernard Shaw and Mrs. Patrick Campbell: Their Correspondence*, ed. Alan Dent (London: Victor Gollancz, 1952), pp. 146–47.
11. Later the word "generation" was changed to "age."
12. Originally, Shaw left the two dead, the soldier and Cauchon, kneeling; but later decided against it.
13. Edmund Wilson, for example, writing in the *New Republic* on 27 August 1924 finds this passage "disconcertingly out of key with the naive faith of the middle ages."
14. J. M. Robertson, *Mr. Shaw and "The Maid"* (London: Richard Cobden-Sanderson, 1925), p. 46.
15. William Searle, *The Saint and the Skeptics: Joan of Arc in the Work of Mark Twain, Anatole France, and Bernard Shaw* (Detroit: Wayne State University Press, 1976), p. 107.
16. G. B. Shaw, "On the Principles that Govern the Dramatist," letter to the *New York Times*, 2 June 1912, reprinted in *Shaw on Theatre*, ed. E. J. West (New York: Hill and Wang, 1958), p. 116.
17. It may seem surprising that the serpent in the Garden of Eden should be chosen to articulate the Shavian viewpoint, unless one realizes that to Shaw temptation and inspiration were one and the same thing.
18. For much of the illustration in the above three paragraphs I am indebted to William Searle's excellent *The Saint and the Skeptics*.
19. In the original shorthand manuscript he is described as having "a touch of the troubadour which gives him some poetic beauty."

20. William Searle, "Shaw's Saint Joan as 'Protestant,'" *Shaw Review* 15, no. 3 (September 1972): pp. 110–16.
21. There seems little reason to suppose that John Corbin's rendering of this line in his *New York Times* review of the first performance "How long, O *God*, how long?" is anything more than mishearing on his part. At no time did Shaw write it thus.

Chapter 6

1. Quoted in Lawrence Langner, *The Magic Curtain* (New York: Dutton, 1951), p. 175.
2. This play was ten years old, and had also premièred in New York on 24 December 1914. It had not been seen before in London.
3. See A. Russell Thorndike, *Sybil Thorndike* (London: Butterworth, 1929), p. 291.
4. Langner, *The Magic Curtain*, p. 177. It is the Theatre Guild's production of Ferenc Molnar's *Liliom* to which Langner is referring.
5. H. Blum, *A Pictorial History of the American Theatre 1900–1956* (New York: Greenberg, 1956), p. 47.
6. She helped found the Civic Repertory Theatre in 1926, and twenty years later, the American Repertory Theatre.
7. Langner to Shaw, quoted in L. Langner *G.B.S. and the Lunatic* (London: Hutchinson, 1964), p. 65.
8. Eva Le Gallienne to the author, 23 September 1978.
9. Langner, *The Magic Curtain*, p. 178.
10. Langner to Shaw, in Langner, *G.B.S.*, p. 65.
11. The play was by H.-R. Lenormand, who was later responsible for the changes to A. Hamon's French script of *Saint Joan* (see note 76 below). Interesting, in view of his adverse review of Shaw's play, is the fact that *The Failures* was directed by Stark Young, the critic.
12. Langner, *The Magic Curtain*, p. 178.
13. Ada Patterson, "Saint Joan Descends from the Shrine: A Frank and Intimate Interview with Winifred Lenihan Who Interprets Shaw's New Heroine," *Theatre Magazine* (New York) 30 (30 June 1924).
14. Ibid.
15. See Norman Hapgood's comments in "My Return to the Stage," *Hearst's International Magazine* 45 (May 1924): 74–77, 156–58.
16. Alice Griffin, "The New York Critics and *Saint Joan*," *Shaw Bulletin*, January 1955.
17. Irving McKee, "Shaw's *Saint Joan* and the American Critics," *The Shavian* 2, no. 8 (February 1964): 13–16.
18. Jack Crawford, "Broadway Is Inspired," *Drama*, 14 February 1924, p. 178.
19. Except for Nathan's review in the *American Mercury* which claimed that Miss Lenihan was so unequal to the heroic demands of the role of Joan that the rest of the cast was plainly concerned with "laboriously playing down to her," and Percy Hammond who described her as "a smug and self-satisfied flapper, eager for excitement." But of the rest, even Stark Young who dwelt on the play's shortcomings, described her performance as good by comparison with most of the actors available for the part, saying "there is sincerity and honesty of intention that is unusual among our young actresses, and that deserves and compels a careful criticism."
20. Crawford, "Broadway Is Inspired," p. 196.
21. Shaw to Langner, quoted in Langner *G.B.S. and the Lunatic*, p. 69.

22. "A Dialogue on Things in General between George Bernard Shaw and Archibald Henderson," *Harper's Magazine*, May 1924.
23. She had previously been presented with a statuette of Saint Joan by a representative of France on the night of the play's transfer from the Garrick to the Empire Theatre.
24. He quoted the circumstance in his battle with the Catholic Action group over his screenplay in the thirties.
25. Shaw to Theresa Helburn, in Langner, *G.B.S. and the Lunatic*, p. 109.
26. Shaw to Langner, quoted in Langner, *The Magic Curtain*, p. 175.
27. Langner, *G.B.S. and the Lunatic*, p. 62.
28. Lee Simonson to Shaw, 30 December 1923, British Library Add. MSS. 50519, vol. 12. Shaw had warned Langner in his letter of 3 December 1923, "Simonson must not make the scenery fantastic." See Langner, *G.B.S. and the Lunatic*, p. 63.
29. Shaw to Langner, in Langner, *The Magic Curtain*, p. 182.
30. Ibid.
31. Lillah McCarthy, O.B.E. (Lady Keeble), *Myself and My Friends* (London: Thornton-Butterworth, 1933), p. 115.
32. Ibid., p. 209.
33. A. Russell Thorndike, *Sybil Thorndike*, p. 291.
34. See Doris Arthur Jones, *The Life and Letters of Henry Arthur Jones* (London: Victor Gollancz, 1930), p. 338.
35. G. B. Shaw, *To a Young Actress: The Letters of Bernard Shaw to Molly Tompkins*, ed. Peter Tompkins (New York: Clarkson N. Potter, 1960), p. 30.
36. Archibald Henderson, "George Bernard Shaw Self Revealed," *Fortnightly Review*, 1 April 1926, p. 612.
37. *Theatre Arts* 33 (August 1949): 6–11.
38. Jack Hawkins, *Anything for a Quiet Life: The Autobiography of Jack Hawkins* (London: Hamish Hamilton, 1973), p. 16. This reveals a curious trick of memory. Shaw, as we know from Henderson's account of him in *Harper's Magazine*, had snow white hair in February 1924.
39. See, for example, John Mason Brown in the *Saturday Review of Literature*, 27 October 1951, who reports Margaret Webster's description of Shaw's marvellous reading of the play to the Thorndike/Casson company, in which Webster was an understudy.
40. Sybil Thorndike (Dame), "Thanks to Bernard Shaw," in Raymond Mander and Joe Mitchenson, *Theatrical Companion to Shaw: A Pictorial Record of the First Performances of the Plays of George Bernard Shaw* (London: Rockliff, Salisbury Square, 1954), p. 13.
41. G. B. Shaw, "Rules for Directors," reprinted in *Shaw on Theatre*, ed. E. J. West (New York: Hill and Wang, 1958), p. 280.
42. Ibid., p. 283.
43. Blanche Patch, *Thirty Years with G.B.S.* (London: Victor Gollancz, 1951), p. 50.
44. E. Ambrose Couch to Shaw, 14 March 1924, British Library Add. MSS. 50519, vol. 12.
45. Shaw to Molly Tompkins, n.d., *To a Young Actress*, p. 62. Richard Huggett in *The Truth about "Pygmalion"* (London: William Heinemann, 1969), p. 81, claims that Ernest Thesiger as the dauphin was the only actor other than Edmond Gurney to receive Shaw's highest accolade of being told that he had nothing to teach him. The British Museum possesses thirty-six pages of these rehearsal notes which begin on 3 March 1924, and conclude on the twenty-fourth. The jottings on each page are short, and most concern matters of emphasis (words underlined that need stressing by individuals), for example, "Lemaître—This girl is not..." or instructions to the entire

company, for example, "All play to noodle." Less frequently, the music of a line is brought out, for example "Stog—and by God cresc ∠ God." And least frequent, but perhaps most interesting, there are suggestions for movement, as for example when on Joan's line "Why do you chain my feet . . . ?" she is instructed to "kick the chair." See British Library Add. MSS. 50644, vol. 137, fols. 131–67.

46. Thorndike, *Sybil Thorndike*, p. 293.
47. Raymond Massey to the author, 18 July 1978.
48. Ibid.
49. Lewis Casson (Sir), "G.B.S. at Rehearsal," in Mander and Mitchenson, *Theatrical Companion*, p. 18.
50. Hawkins, *A Quiet Life*, pp. 19–20.
51. Thorndike, *Sybil Thorndike*, p. 293.
52. Lillah McCarthy, *Myself and My Friends*, p. 115.
53. See particularly Craig's response to Henderson's *Table Talk of G.B.S.* (London: Chapman and Hall, 1925), which appeared in his magazine *Mask* 12 (January 1926), under the title "The Colossus. G.B.S."
54. G. B. Shaw, "The Colossus Speaks," originally published in *Mask* 12 (April 1926); reprinted in *Shaw on Theatre*, ed. E. J. West, p. 175.
55. Ibid.
56. Ibid., p. 176.
57. "Joan of Arc and Mr. Shaw," *Daily Mirror*, 27 March 1924.
58. Thorndike, *Sybil Thorndike*, p. 294.
59. A. B. Walkley, "Saint Joan. Sancta Simplicitas. Anatole France's Story," *The Times* (London), 26 March 1924. This is presumably the piece erroneously referred to by Hesketh Pearson as "a long article against a work he had neither seen nor read, protesting that the subject was far too solemn and serious to be dealt with by a playwright of Shaw's description." Pearson exaggerates. Only three or four sentences in the article refer to Shaw at all; and in these Walkley expresses misgivings merely, adding "I can only hope my misgivings will prove to have done him an injustice."
60. Archibald Henderson, *George Bernard Shaw: Man of the Century* (New York: Appleton-Century-Crofts, 1956), p. 600.
61. Sir John Gielgud, preface to Sheridan Morley's *Sybil Thorndike: A Life in the Theatre* (London: Weidenfeld and Nicolson, 1977), p. 9.
62. G. B. Shaw to Lawrence Langner, quoted in Langner, *G.B.S. and the Lunatic*, p. 76.
63. Ibid.
64. Desmond MacCarthy, "St. Joan," *New Statesman*, 12 April 1924, p. 14; rpt. in *"Saint Joan" Fifty Years After*, ed. Stanley Weintraub (Baton Rouge: Louisiana State University Press, 1973).
65. R. Ellis Roberts, "*Saint Joan* by Bernard Shaw. At the New Theatre," *Bookman*, May 1924, p. 140.
66. See Patch, *Thirty Years*, p. 52.
67. See Henderson, *George Bernard Shaw*, p. 600.
68. L. Alma Tadema to Shaw, n.d., British Library Add. MSS. 50519, vol. 12.
69. See below, note 84.
70. G. B. Shaw, *Era* (London), 10 January 1934.
71. J. C. Trewin, *Sybil Thorndike: An Illustrated Study of Dame Sybil's Work with a List of Her Appearances on Stage and Screen*, Theatre World Monograph, no. 4 (London: Rockliff, Salisbury Square, 1955), pp. 59–60.
72. James Graham, "Shaw on *Saint Joan*," *New York Times*, 13 April 1924; rpt. in *"Saint Joan" Fifty Years After*, ed. S. Weintraub.

73. Aniouta Pitoëff, *Ludmilla ma mère: vie de Ludmilla et de Georges Pitoëff* (Paris: Julliard, 1955), p. 232. My translation.
74. Daniel C. Gerould, *"Saint Joan* in Paris," *Shaw Review* 7 (January 1964): 11–23; rpt. in *"Saint Joan"* Fifty Years After.
75. See Patch, *Thirty Years*, p. 66.
76. William Searle in *The Saint and the Skeptics: Joan of Arc in the Work of Mark Twain, Anatole France, and Bernard Shaw* (Detroit: Wayne State University Press, 1976), p. 168, cites Shaw's alterations to the Hamons' text which are to be found in the "Sainte Jeanne" typescript at the Academic Centre Library, University of Texas.
77. See Gerould, *"Saint Joan* in Paris," p. 15.
78. Pitoëff, *Ludmilla,* p. 230.
79. Henri-René Lenormand, *Les Pitoëff: souvenirs* (Paris: Odette Lieutier, 1943), pp. 121–22.
80. Pitoëff, *Ludmilla,* p. 224. My translation. The set was an exciting one, conceived under the influence of the Cubists; and the idea of all the action in *Saint Joan* revolving around a triptych was a natural progression from the Pitoëffs' desire to make Jeanne herself the centre, and to make her saintliness *her* centre.
81. Ibid., p. 233. My translation.
82. Shaw, *To a Young Actress,* p. 88.
83. Frank Harris, *Bernard Shaw: An Unauthorised Biography Based on Firsthand Information,* With a Postscript by Mr. Shaw (London: Gollancz, 1931), p. 287. Shaw had made fun of Bernstein in the pages of *Le Temps.* When Ludmilla played the part in 1930 Herbert Farjeon in the *Graphic* contrasted her tranquil peasant beauty with Thorndike's "impetuous, bucolic, gee-up—Dobbin opening" likening her, in her spiritual loveliness to the great Duse. But finally, like Shaw, he gave the palm to Sybil Thorndike saying that Mme Pitoëff was never a leader "...if she was a depth...she was never a force." H. Farjeon, "The London Stage," *Graphic* (London) 128 (21 June 1930): 654.
84. G. B. Shaw, "Shaw Unperturbed by Immortality," replies to a questionnaire by Leslie Rees, *Era* (London), 10 January 1934.
85. S. Trebitsch, "A Visit to Bernard Shaw," from *Vossische Zeitung,* reprinted in *Living Age* 320 (2 February 1924): 221.
86. Ibid., p. 223.
87. Shaw to editor of the *New York Times,* 14 September 1936, p. 14f.
88. Shaw to Molly Tompkins, in Shaw, *To a Young Actress,* p. 87. Emma Grammatica was the Italian Saint Joan.
89. G. B. Shaw, *Translations and Tomfooleries* (London: Constable & Co., 1932), p. 6.
90. Ibid., p. 5.
91. See British Library Add. MSS. 50519, vol. 12.
92. Robert Benchley, "Vienna Letter," "Drama," *Life* 86 (20 August 1925): 18.
93. See British Library Add. MSS. 50519, vol. 12, letter from Harry Toogood, Third House of Trade Union, Sovietsky Place, Moscow, USSR, 11 February 1925.
94. "Soviet Fooled London on Shaw; Didn't Stop His Play 'Saint Joan.'" Special cable to the *New York Times,* 7 February 1925, p. 17: 2.
95. "Life Letters and the Arts," *Living Age* (Boston) 329 (8 May 1926).
96. Ibid.
97. See *Graphic,* 11 September 1926.
98. Paul Scheffer, report in the *Berliner Tageblatt,* 16 May 1926, reprinted as "Theatres That Are Different," *Living Age* (Boston) 330 (14 September 1926): 505.

Chapter 7

1. It is strange that on 16 April 1924, when advertising the Lane reprint of Anatole France's *The Life of Joan of Arc*, a book that Shaw was to dismiss in his Preface, the publishers praised the French book by quoting a line of praise from, of all places, *The Times'* review of Shaw's play!

2. For example, on 7 September 1923 Father Leonard sent Shaw a copy of the *Acta Apostolicae Sedis* (containing an official account of the last steps taken in the canonization of Joan); and on 16 October of the same year Julius Bertram sent Shaw a book-list which included Harriet Parr's *Jeanne d'Arc: Life and Death*, 2 vols. (1866). See British Library Add. MSS. 50519, vol. 12.

3. G. B. Shaw, British Library Add. MSS. 45923, fol. 73.

4. Ibid., fol. 92.

5. Ibid. The reference to cremation is interesting: Shaw became a life member of the Cremation Society of England on 28 April 1924, while he was writing the Preface.

6. Mr. Kuntz to Shaw, 30 November 1923, British Library Add. MSS. 50519, vol. 12.

7. Ibid.

8. G. B. Shaw, British Library Add. MSS. 45923, fol. 95.

9. S. W. Dyde, "Shakespeare in the Eyes of Bernard Shaw," *Queen's Quarterly* 32 (January/March 1925): 276–84.

10. John C. Blankenagel, "Shaw's *Saint Joan* and Schiller's *Jungfrau von Orleans*," *Journal of English and Germanic Philology* 25 (July 1926): 379–92.

11. W. A. Oldfather, "Mr. Shaw and the *Apology* of Socrates," *Classical Journal* 21 (January 1926): 286–90.

12. Arnold Lunn, "The Inquisition and Mr. Bernard Shaw," *Review of the Churches* 3 (January 1926): 77–88.

13. Werner Jung, *La Jeanne d'Arc de Bernard Shaw* (Brussels: La Renaissance de l'Occident, 1925); J. M. Robertson, *Mr. Shaw and "The Maid"* (London: Richard Cobden-Sanderson, 1925).

14. Florence Hardy to Shaw, 29 June 1924, British Library Add. MSS. 50519, vol. 12.

15. John Drinkwater to Shaw, 7 August 1924, ibid.

16. Laurence Binyon to Shaw, 3 July 1924, ibid.

17. Stanley Weintraub, *Bernard Shaw*, in *Anglo-Irish Literature: A Review of Research*, ed. Richard J. Finneran (New York: Modern Language Association, 1978).

18. G. B. Shaw, in "The Table-Talk of G.B.S.," *Harper's*, May 1924.

19. Blankenagel, "Shaw's *Saint Joan*," pp. 390–91.

20. Jung, *La Jeanne d'Arc de Bernard Shaw*, p. 23.

21. G. S. Fraser, *The Modern Writer and His World: Continuity and Innovation in Twentieth Century Literature* (New York: Frederick Praeger, 1953, 1964), p. 196.

22. A. Obraztsova, "A People's Heroine," from *Dramatturgicheskii Metod Bernarda Shou* (Moscow, 1965), translated by Kaaren Page and adapted by Stanley Weintraub in *"Saint Joan" Fifty Years After: 1923/24–1973/74* (Baton Rouge: Louisiana State University Press, 1973), p. 225.

23. R. (Bonar) Law, "Mr. Shaw, God and Saint Joan," *Outlook* 53 (14 June 1924): 410.

24. H. Lüdeke, "Some Remarks on Shaw's History Plays," *English Studies*, October 1955, p. 244.

25. S. H. Butcher, *Aristotle's Theory of Poetry and Fine Art, with a Critical Text and Translation of the Poetics* (London: Macmillan, 1932) quoted in Louis L. Martz "The Saint as Tragic Hero: *Saint Joan* and *Murder in the Cathedral*," from Cleanth Brooks,

ed., *Tragic Themes in Western Literature* (New Haven: Yale University Press, 1955), p. 151.

26. Ibid., p. 156.
27. Ibid., p. 158.
28. Ibid., pp. 158–60.
29. Sylvan Barnet, "Bernard Shaw on Tragedy," *Publications of the Modern Language Association*, 1956, p. 899. My italics.
30. G. B. Shaw, from *Dramatic Heritage*, quoted in Barnet, above.
31. Gerald C. Weales, *Religion in Modern English Drama* (Philadelphia: University of Pennsylvania Press, 1961), p. 74.
32. S. John Macksoud and Ross Altman, "Voices in Opposition: A Burkeian Rhetoric of *Saint Joan*," *Quarterly Journal of Speech* 57 (April 1971): 144.
33. Frederic T. Wood, "Individualism in Religious Thought in the Plays of Ibsen and Bernard Shaw," *Calcutta Review*, series 3 (June 1935), p. 247.
34. Allardyce Nicoll, *World Drama from Aeschylus to Anouilh* (New York: Harcourt Brace & World, n.d.), p. 862.
35. Among these writers are the American John Balderston, in whose *Berkeley Square* (1926) a man of today is spirited back into the eighteenth century; and Maurice Colbourne, whose play *Charles the King* was first presented at the Lyric Theatre, Shaftsbury Avenue, London, on 9 October 1936, with Colbourne himself in the part of the Earl of Stafford. This play bears the imprint of *Saint Joan* (in the first production of which, Colbourne, one remembers, played Dunois) in its division into short scenes, the deliberate modernity of dialogue, and in the author's reminder that "Charles the King is not primarily a 'period play' but has a message for this troubled century." M. Colbourne, *Charles the King* (London: Samuel French, 1937), p. 10.
36. Shaw to Frank Harris, 20 May 1926, quoted in Harris, *Bernard Shaw: An Unauthorised Biography* (London: Gollancz, 1931), p. 350.
37. Ibid., p. 351.
38. Lord Alfred Douglas to Shaw, 19 November 1931, British Library Add. MSS. 50533.
39. Louis Crompton, *Shaw the Dramatist* (Lincoln: University of Nebraska Press, 1969), p. 199.
40. Martz, "The Saint as Tragic Hero," pp. 164–65, 175.
41. Notwithstanding Nicoll's comment quoted in the text, p. 109. It still seems to me that J. H. Buckland was more prophetic when, in praising Shaw's method of treating history, he stated: "Yet its very familiarity will make it but the easier to learn the lesson taught by Mr. Shaw and may encourage the application of his method to other stories and other epochs." Buckland, "Saint Joan," *History*, January 1925, p. 287.
42. D. Knowles, *French Drama of the Inter-War Years 1919–1939* (London: George Harrap and Co., 1967), p. 282.
43. Hugh Allison Smith, *Main Currents of Modern French Drama* (New York: Henry Holt and Co., 1925), p. 302.
44. Paul Surer, *Cinquante ans de théâtre*, Société d'Edition D'Enseignement Supérieure (Paris: 5 Place de la Sorbonne, 1969), p. 12.
45. Harold Hobson, *The French Theatre of Today: An English View* (New York: Benjamin Blom, 1953; rpt. 1965), p. 39.
46. Ibid.
47. Beatrix Dussane, *Notes de théâtre*, quoted in Hobson above, note 45.
48. Robert Cohen, *Giraudoux: Three Faces of Destiny* (Chicago: University of Chicago Press, 1968), p. 7.

49. See Jacques Guichard, *Modern French Theatre from Giraudoux to Beckett* (New Haven: Yale University Press, 1961), p. 14.

50. Cohen, *Giraudoux*, p. 138.

51. Karl-Heinz Schoeps, "Epic Structures in the Plays of Bernard Shaw and Bertolt Brecht," in *Essays on Brecht: Theatre and Politics*, ed. Siegfried Mews and Herbert Knust (Chapel Hill: University of North Carolina Press, 1974), p. 29.

52. John Fuegi, *The Essential Brecht* (Los Angeles: Hennessey and Ingalls, 1972), p. 207n1.

53. Ibid., p. 211.

54. Schoeps, "Epic Structures," p. 32.

55. Ibid., p. 43.

56. F. G. Barker, "A Man for All Seasons," *Plays and Players* 8, no. 5 (February 1961), p. 13.

57. Ruth W. Sedgwick, "*Saint Joan*," *Stage* 13 (April 1936): 31.

58. See Lawrence Langner, *The Magic Curtain* (New York: Dutton, 1951), p. 411.

59. *Saint Joan. A Screenplay by Bernard Shaw*, edited and with an Introduction by Bernard F. Dukore (Seattle: University of Washington Press, 1968).

60. Val Gielgud, "Bernard Shaw and the Radio," in S. Winsten, *G.B.S. at 90* (New York: Dodd, Mead and Co., 1946), p. 229.

61. St. John Ervine to Shaw, 16 September 1941, British Library Add. MSS. 50533.

62. L. C. Lloyd, "On the Air," *Spectator* 178 (13 June 1947): 685.

63. F.S., "St. Joan," *Theatre World* 44 (January 1948): 10.

64. *Plays and Players*, however, described her as "a small domesticated Joan who would have been much happier at the kitchen sink peeling potatoes than fighting with an army on the banks of the Loire." "No Thrill in Fame," *Plays and Players* 1, no. 10 (July 1954).

65. Stanley Weintraub tells us of the enthusiastic response of the Nobel Prize Committee's resident expert Per Hallstrom. See S. Weintraub, "The Genesis of *Saint Joan*," *Literatur in Wissenschaft und Unterricht* 10 (1977): 271.

66. Preston Benson, "GBS — Man and Superman," *Star* (London), 30 November 1950, p. 5.

67. G. B. Shaw, *Bernard Shaw's Rhyming Picture Guide to Ayot Saint Lawrence* (Luton: Leagrave Press, 1950), p. 2.

Index